MEDIA AND COMMUNICATIONS - TECHNOLOGIES, POLICIES AND CHALLENGES

SOCIAL MEDIA

GLOBAL PERSPECTIVES, APPLICATIONS AND BENEFITS AND DANGERS

MEDIA AND COMMUNICATIONS - TECHNOLOGIES, POLICIES AND CHALLENGES

Additional books in this series can be found on Nova's website under the Series tab.

Additional e-books in this series can be found on Nova's website under the e-book tab.

MEDIA AND COMMUNICATIONS - TECHNOLOGIES, POLICIES AND CHALLENGES

SOCIAL MEDIA

GLOBAL PERSPECTIVES, APPLICATIONS AND BENEFITS AND DANGERS

ANNMARIE BENNET
EDITOR

New York

Copyright © 2015 by Nova Science Publishers, Inc.

All rights reserved. No part of this book may be reproduced, stored in a retrieval system or transmitted in any form or by any means: electronic, electrostatic, magnetic, tape, mechanical photocopying, recording or otherwise without the written permission of the Publisher.

For permission to use material from this book please contact us:
nova.main@novapublishers.com

NOTICE TO THE READER

The Publisher has taken reasonable care in the preparation of this book, but makes no expressed or implied warranty of any kind and assumes no responsibility for any errors or omissions. No liability is assumed for incidental or consequential damages in connection with or arising out of information contained in this book. The Publisher shall not be liable for any special, consequential, or exemplary damages resulting, in whole or in part, from the readers' use of, or reliance upon, this material. Any parts of this book based on government reports are so indicated and copyright is claimed for those parts to the extent applicable to compilations of such works.

Independent verification should be sought for any data, advice or recommendations contained in this book. In addition, no responsibility is assumed by the publisher for any injury and/or damage to persons or property arising from any methods, products, instructions, ideas or otherwise contained in this publication.

This publication is designed to provide accurate and authoritative information with regard to the subject matter covered herein. It is sold with the clear understanding that the Publisher is not engaged in rendering legal or any other professional services. If legal or any other expert assistance is required, the services of a competent person should be sought. FROM A DECLARATION OF PARTICIPANTS JOINTLY ADOPTED BY A COMMITTEE OF THE AMERICAN BAR ASSOCIATION AND A COMMITTEE OF PUBLISHERS.

Additional color graphics may be available in the e-book version of this book.

LIBRARY OF CONGRESS CATALOGING-IN-PUBLICATION DATA

ISBN: 978-1-63463-175-4

Published by Nova Science Publishers, Inc. † New York

CONTENTS

PREFACE

The prevalence of social media avails individual users and organizations with unprecedented access to personal information that was once arduous to gather. Undoubtedly, privacy concerns on social media platforms become critically important as vendors can now potentially have access to a large collection of users' personal information. This book discusses the privacy concerns in using social media. It discusses the negative impact social media has on different populations; the use of social media for job placement; the dangers of social media for the psyche; and videos as a form of transmedia storytelling.

Chapter 1 – Privacy concerns associated with the use of social media applications is gaining significant interest both in the academic and organizational communities. Calls have been made to researchers to investigate the theoretical underpinnings that explain concerns for information privacy in the social media context. A review of the information privacy literature reveals that till date, no study has taken a theory-driven approach to understand privacy concerns in the social media context. To fill the gap in the literature, this article evaluates information privacy concern instrument from prior research in the social media context. This Chapter draws on Social Penetration theory and Communication Privacy Management theory to explain social media users' information privacy concern (SMIPC). Drawing on a sample of 270 avid social media users, this study examines the factor structure of the dimensions of concern for information privacy instrument from prior research. An exploratory factor analysis followed by a confirmatory factor analysis revealed three first-order factor structure of social media users' concern for information privacy measurement instrument. Further analysis of alternative factor models revealed that a second order factor structure of

SMIPC performs better than its first-order factor structure in the social media context.

Chapter 2 – Social media is said to be one way to disseminate health information. With the proliferation of social media tools, such as Facebook, Twitter, Tumblr, and YouTube, more millennials are engaged in health information seeking and discovery. To develop targeted health messages to this demographic, web-based applications and social media tools informed by millennials' perceptions can be effective. Prior research has shown that social media can be effective in dampening the stigma associated with health conditions, such as HIV, even in cases where consumers simply engage in health information seeking behaviors. The authors use the Extended Parallel Process Model (EPPM) of behavior change communication to examine specifically how Black college-aged and matriculating women perceive the threat of HIV and their ability to prevent transmission. The purpose of this study is to assess perceived threat and perceived efficacy via the EPPM in order to inform the ongoing social media development of HIV prevention messages for myHealthImpactNetwork.org, an online experience targeting Black women. A convenience sample of 49 Black women was recruited and invited to complete both paper and pencil, and online surveys. Overall, the sample had positive EPPM scores, meaning that the participants perceived HIV as a severe threat to which they feel mildly susceptible, but very capable of preventing. The sample respondents' positive EPPM scores indicate that messages targeting this group should continue to stress the severity of HIV and their susceptibility to the disease as well as strategies to prevent its transmission. Thus, tailored fear appeals can offer an effective messaging approach to communicating the threat of HIV to this population. These results offer insights into how social media can be used, consumed and perceived among diverse populations.

Chapter 3 – The process of interaction between individuals, through the use of social media, is one of the most complex problems that theorists have had to analyze in recent years. Social media tools are becoming an important presence in recruitment processes, transforming them. Today many organizations are facing a challenge: they have to make choices in order to allow their operators to use this new method of communication with their students and with firms or forbid it. The rapid changes that the diffusion of social media has had in the communication processes would undoubtedly impose a drastic change: the use of social media allow an instant sharing of ideas, opinions, knowledge and experiences, creating a new "space-time" dimension that could be translated in a new way (additional) to "recruit" workers. Although there are a lot of benefits and promises from social media, however several risks are associated with their use. The ambiguity related to legal and ethical issues (for example individual privacy) of social media, at the same time, contains the enthusiasm related to the potentialities that social media offer. In particular this chapter aims at analyzing the perceived risks and benefits of social media in job placement offices of Universities in four countries (Italy, Switzerland, Austria and Germany) and at providing an analysis of the phenomenon of social recruitment in Universities: it will be done through the analysis of the use of this instrument for the placement of graduates in companies. It can be useful for university managers and for firms to understand whether the presence of Universities on social media by students and firms is positive or not.

Chapter 4 – This chapter examines how individual users of social media characteristically represent themselves online. It considers whether the process and opportunity for the (apparently) controlled representation of the self online i.e., via the self-selection of favourable visual 'show' material and favourable written 'tell' material, actually has the inherent potential to affect the psyche of the individual and thus represent danger. In doing so, this chapter effectively asks to what extent an improved awareness of the potential for social media to affect the psyche, should actually be the conscious concern of all. The process of online representation is cumulative, and with respect to social media, effectively creates a socially derived and socially driven, composite online image known as a social avatar. Humans notably select their best aspects for presentation to others, and the self-rendered nature of the social avatar can be seen to reflect this evolutionary tendency, to the extent that social avatars effectively facilitate a psychologically significant *'gap'* between the online image of an individual (as a hoped for '*representation'* of the self) and their offline identity (as the real '*substance'* of the self). Social avatars are therefore an important phenomenon to recognise. They function as a simple but effective facilitation mechanism, by which the effects of using social media are delivered to the psyche (including shifts in identity and even psychopathology). Additionally, social avatars have value in the research setting (e.g., they can be dissected to examine levels of narcissism), and conceptual value in the ongoing quest to understand the complicated directional pathways and relationships between social media and the psyche. This chapter therefore provides a timely overview of the dangers of social media for the psyche and examines the implications for good mental health in the age of cyberspace. It highlights the pervasive influence of social media on identity formation and youth aspiration, and considers the range of negative psychological transformations which can occur. This chapter also raises awareness of what can be an insidious process of psychological erosion, with important human needs such as privacy, authenticity and personal integration, sacrificed along the way - and all with a potential net cost to well-being. In order to achieve an overview (and in a likely reflection of the sprawling nature of social networks themselves), this chapter references a wide range of material including academic research, media commentary, and a selection of the many valuable personal viewpoints which exist 'hidden-away' online.

Chapter 5 – Fan vids are an emergent form of storytelling in the current social media epoch. As a genre of works, they comprise montages of visual material culled from mass media source texts and set to music through the grassroots practice of vidding. As vidders search, cull, and edit movie images, they recast the cinematic stories by decontextualizing the source materials and extending the frontier of the narrative to other signifying realms. Vidding could be said to constitute a grassroots, fan-driven form of transmedia storytelling, by which the integral elements of a fiction are systematically dispersed across multiple media platforms. *The Matrix*, a celebrated Hollywood science fiction franchise, has inspired many such instances of transmedia storytelling, demonstrating how the story is retold by ordinary fans as they transpose movie images from cinematic space to cyberspace. This essay focuses on two fan vids from YouTube, the most popular video-sharing site, entitled "I, Neo (Mos Def / Massive Attack / Matrix Mashup)" and "Matrix Vs. Excision & Downlink - Existence VIP Dub Mashup" to examine how vidders incorporate new content to expand and alter the *Matrix* narrative into the bottom-up generated content. When *Matrix* footage is eclectically cut to electronic music, Neo's story is no longer represented and understood within a fixed symbolic system, but rather in a hybrid, open framework, allowing for diverse directionality of interpretation. While transmedia storytelling conventions stress that all components from all media should cohere with a consistent narrative world, *The Matrix* story in these fan vids is embellished by insinuating a narrative rupture. The vids allow a narrative experience which is fragmented, inconsistent, or even disintegrated, partaking of a postmodernist discourse. Although *The Matrix*'s original allusions to messianic-redemptive Christian mythology, of particular interest for my analysis, remain apparent in these vids, the vidders have obscured, altered, and reworked the cinematic story, concomitantly generating new stories. Fan vids open up new possibilities for re-presenting and re-interpreting media texts, posing both challenges and opportunities for the practices of storytelling and meaning-making in the global mediascape.

In: Social Media
Editor: Annmarie Bennet

ISBN: 978-1-63463-175-4
© 2015 Nova Science Publishers, Inc.

Chapter 1

AN INSTRUMENT FOR MEASURING SOCIAL MEDIA USERS' INFORMATION PRIVACY CONCERNS

Babajide Osatuyi*
University of Texas-Pan American
College of Business Administration
Department of Computer Information Systems
& Quantitative Methods, Texas, US

ABSTRACT

Privacy concerns associated with the use of social media applications is gaining significant interest both in the academic and organizational communities. Calls have been made to researchers to investigate the theoretical underpinnings that explain concerns for information privacy in the social media context. A review of the information privacy literature reveals that till date, no study has taken a theory-driven approach to understand privacy concerns in the social media context. To fill the gap in the literature, this article evaluates information privacy concern instrument from prior research in the social media context. This Chapter draws on Social Penetration theory and Communication Privacy Management theory to explain social media users' information privacy concern (SMIPC). Drawing on a sample of 270 avid social media users,

* osatuyib@utpa.edu.

this study examines the factor structure of the dimensions of concern for information privacy instrument from prior research. An exploratory factor analysis followed by a confirmatory factor analysis revealed three first-order factor structure of social media users' concern for information privacy measurement instrument. Further analysis of alternative factor models revealed that a second order factor structure of SMIPC performs better than its first-order factor structure in the social media context.

Keywords: Privacy concerns, social media, instrument development, information privacy, validity, confirmatory factor analysis, exploratory factor analysis

INTRODUCTION

The prevalence of social media avail individual users and organizations with unprecedented access to personal information that was once arduous to gather. Undoubtedly, privacy concerns on social media platforms become critically important as vendors can now potentially have access to a large collection of users' personal information. Unlike other online applications, users voluntarily contribute their personal information on social media platforms [1], thereby increasing the ease of gathering personally identifiable information.

Information privacy in the information systems (IS) literature is conceptualized in terms of personal information gathering, sharing, and usage [2, 3]. However, researchers need to consider taking a broader perspective with the definition of information privacy, especially in the context of social media [1, 4]. Information privacy on social media platforms need to be conceptualized as a multi-agent phenomenon that involves the volunteer of personal information from individuals to a group or collective under the assumption that shared information will be kept confidential among agents—social ties, social media platform, and policy makers [1]. Hence, *information privacy* is formally conceptualized in this article as the exchange of personal information among members of a social network with the implicit anticipation that members share a responsibility of keeping the shared information private (Osatuyi, forthcoming).

In addition to users' shared responsibility to protect self-disclosed personal information, social media platforms provide policies, interfaces, and features that structure interaction among users, as well as to third parties on how to provide add-on features and applications to extend the platform's functionality [5].

Researchers call for "theoretical and operational assumptions underlying the structure of constructs such as concern for information privacy (CFIP) should be re-investigated in light of emerging technology, practice, and research [6, p.37]." Drawing on Communication Privacy Management (CPM) theory [7], this article proposes that social media users' information privacy concerns can be characterized in terms of access to personal information, errors in storing personal information, and collection of personal information. CPM provides coordination rules for information owners to collectively manage the disclosure of personal information.

In response to calls to study information privacy concerns in the context of social interactions [1], this study seeks to develop an instrument that can predict and explain information disclosure practices on social media platforms. In this study, social media information privacy concern (SMIPC) is defined as concerns about loss of privacy as a result of the disclosure of personal information to known and unknown external agents—including other social media users, social media platforms, and third parties.

This article contributes to the information privacy literature by providing a re-conceptualization of a broader perspective of information privacy on social media platforms, the development and empirical validation of a measurement instrument for studying users' information privacy concerns on social media platforms.

Theoretical Background Current Information Privacy Concern Measurement Instruments

One of the major breakthroughs in information privacy research was a study conducted by Smith et al. [3]. In their work, they found that concern for information privacy was influenced by four fundamental factors based on individuals' concern in response to organizations' information practices, namely collection, unauthorized secondary use (internal and external), improper access to personal information, and errors in personal information storage. Smith et al. [3] measured and validated the four factors as first-order constructs in a nomological network.

In a later validation of Smith et al.'s [3] model, Stewart and Segars [6] posited that CFIP is complex and should be measured as a second-order construct. Stewart and Segars [6] then developed, tested, and validated their proposed hypothesis with CFIP as a multi-dimensional construct in a nomological network and found that it mediated the relationship between computer anxiety and behavioral intentions. Since then, researchers have validated the use of CFIP as a second-order construct, in nomological models across different contexts. While the context of CFIP was on direct offline marketing, Malhotra et al. [8] developed a multi-dimensional scale to measure Internet Users' Information Privacy Concern (IUIPC) in the context of the Internet.

In response to Stewart and Segar's [6] call to investigate the shifting dimensions of information privacy concerns in light of emerging technology, practice, and research, Xu et al. [9, p.3] developed a 9-item instrument to measure mobile users' concerns for information privacy. The research program through which this study is conducted responds to the same call as it investigates measurement scales needed to understand individuals' concern for information privacy on social media platforms, which is increasingly becoming an important communication medium for users, organizations, and government entities.

Communication Privacy Management Theory

Privacy concerns about information sharing and collection is particularly germane to the social media context as users voluntarily generate and contribute their personal information on social media platforms. Users' perception that their personal information may be accessed and used by other entities (i.e., other users, social media platforms, and third-party vendors), may trigger concern for security and privacy. Web 2.0 technologies such as social media platforms are data-driven requiring regular collection of users' preferences, conversations, and personal information in order to improve users' experience on their platform. Users, platform developers, and third party vendors therefore share the ownership and responsibility to ensure that personal information exchanged on social media platforms are kept private [1]. In agreement with Xu et al.'s [9, p.3] notion in their research on mobile users' concern for information privacy, "concerns about personal information disclosure [on social media platforms] cannot be fully understood without knowing users' expectations about how their disclosed information will be used and who will have access to the information."

This article draws on Communication Privacy Management (CPM) theory for its suitability in understanding the privacy consideration for how information is exchanged on social media platforms [7]. CPM is especially useful in this context as it recognizes individual and collective ramifications of information exchanged on social media platforms. It also accounts for the need to establish and coordinate boundaries to manage the privacy of information shared among entities (i.e., users, social media platforms, and vendors). Although CPM was developed before the emergence of social media as a widespread communication tool, this study extends it to account for communication beyond a user and other users, but to include the social media platform provider and other third parties.

CPM is positioned as a rule-based theory which posits that individuals develop rules to determine if and how to share information as a function of five criteria [7]: gender, culture, motivations, risk-benefit assessment, and context. Once individuals decide to disclose their personal information, the information moves to a collective domain where collectives (i.e., users, social media platforms, third parties) manage mutually held privacy boundaries. CPM is mainly focused on the collective management of private information. This focus leads to the need for boundary coordination process to collectively control private information by all the agents in the information space i.e., users, social media platforms, and third parties [7]. CPM theory [7] identifies three boundary rules for coordinating information disclosure between agents, including coordinating permeability rules, coordinating ownership rules, and coordinating linkage rules. These coordination rules "illustrate the modes of change for the dialectic of privacy-disclosure as managed in a collective manner" [7, p.127].

Finally, CPM posit that boundary turbulence occurs when co-owners of information are unable to collectively exhibit coordination rules guiding information permeability, ownership, and linkages [7]. The intervention of the Federal Trade Commission requiring Facebook to withdraw proposed privacy changes that would allow the company to use the names, images, and content of Facebook users for advertising without users' consent is an example of boundary turbulence [10].

Boundary turbulence increases users' privacy concern, consequently leading to re-coordination of their boundary rules to manage information permeability, ownership, and linkages.

Social Media Information Privacy Concern (SMIPC)

Based on the theoretical perspective presented using CPM, four main constructs for measuring users' concern for information privacy on social media platforms are introduced, including 1) unauthorized access and secondary used of personal information—information access, 2) information collection—collection, and 3) erroneous storage and representation of personal information—errors.

Information Access and Use

For research in the information privacy domain, Smith et al. [3] developed two scales (unauthorized access and secondary use) that relate to the use of users' personal information without their consent. *Secondary use* is the use of personal data collected by an organization for a legitimate reason (e.g., shipping information by an e-commerce company), but used for a secondary purpose without the consent of the user. U*nauthorized access* describes the interception of personal information captured from a legitimate transaction by a third party without the consent of either the user or the organization. In the context of social media, secondary use and unauthorized access both describe access and use of personal information without receiving permission from the information owner(s). In accordance to CPM, the unauthorized access and use of users' personal information triggers the coordination of linkage rules used as response mechanism for "the establishment of mutually agreed-upon privacy rules used to choose others who may be privy to the collectively held information [11, p.70]." Drawing on secondary use and unauthorized access dimensions of CFIP, this article posits information access may be important to characterize SMIPC. Information access is conceptualized in the social media context to relate to the access and use of users' personal information without the consent of the user.

Collection

Collection is defined in the information privacy research stream as "concern that extensive amounts of personally identifiable data are being collected and stored in databases [3, p.172]." In today's data-driven society, aggressive data collection strategies are used by various organizations to build a better understanding of their customers as well as to maintain competitive advantage. However, as noted by several researchers [3, 8], the practice of data collection, justifiable or not, raises privacy concerns for customers. With minimal integration into one's daily routine, social media applications may be used to track and gather an individual's behavioral pattern throughout each day e.g., choice of lunch locations, favorite online radio playlist, running/walking route information sharing with friends etc.

Users may not use social media for the fear that their personal information and private conversations may be collected and stored for future business or intelligence analysis. The act of data collection initiates users' tendency to activate their coordination of permeability rules, which Petronio [12] describes as the extent to which information within the collectively owned privacy boundary should be disclosed to others. Studies show report that when individuals are provided with a significant control over information disclosure, they create boundary structures that reduce the amount of information collection by others or they establish boundaries with low permeability [12, 13]. Accordingly, this research posits that personal information collection is an important factor that characterizes SMIPC.

ERRORS

Smith et al. [3, p.172] described error as individuals' "concern that protections against deliberate and accidental errors in personal data are inadequate." The authors noted that privacy-related concerns are initiated when errors are made in the representation of customers' information. In the offline context, such errors are not uncommon due to inevitable mistakes with the data entry process. However, in the context of social media where personal information is user-generated, errors may be conceptualized as a deliberate act on the part of the information provider. Studies abound in the social interaction context that shows that users deliberately enter incomplete or inaccurate information about themselves on online social platforms [e.g., 14]. Using CPM as a backdrop, the tendency for users to provide erroneous information is consistent with ownership coordination strategy [or rules] used by individuals to ensure that unwanted agents are not privy to their complete personal information. From the perspective of the social media platform, improper update of personal information may also lead to erroneous personal data. Lastly, third party vendors have no way of confirming the integrity of consumers' information available to them, which may lead to misappropriation of advertisement or other services. Hence, this study posits that errors characterize SMIPC as it can affect the user, the platform provider, and third party vendors.

METHOD

Scale Development

A survey instrument was developed to test the hypothesized model in accordance to the practice in the information privacy domain [3, 15]. Scales from the instruments for measuring concern for information privacy posited Smith et al. [3] were adapted based on prior research. *Information access* was measured by a combination of items from *unauthorized access* and *secondary use* scales from Smith et al. [3]. *Collection* and *error* were adapted from Smith et al. [3] and measured with multiple items on five-point Likert scales, anchored with strongly disagree to strongly agree. *Behavioral intentions* and *computer anxiety* were adapted from Stewart and Segar's [6] and measured with three items on five-point Likert scales, anchored with highly likely to not at all likely and strongly disagree to strongly agree respectively.

Experts in both social media and information privacy research fields reviewed the initial versions of the survey questions. Additional feedback was received from a sample of graduate and undergraduate students on the clarity of the questions and options before the final version was finally developed. All measurement items used in this research are included in the Appendix.

Survey Design

An online survey was developed and the link was sent to college students in a southern region of United States. Students received extra-credits toward their final grade for participating in the study. To protect the privacy of participants and in compliance with the IRB regulations of the institution, no personally identifiable information was collected from participants. There were 310 participants in the study, but only 250 of the responses were complete and useful for analysis. Respondents had a median age of 19, and 63.2% of them were female. 91% of the participants reported that they use social media on a daily basis. Based on Pew research reports [16], college students are predominant social media users, hence, choosing college students as the study population is ideal for this research.

Data Analysis and Results

Data analysis was conducted in two phases; Phase 1 sought to identify and validate the factor structure of SMIPC and Phase 2 evaluated SMIPC in a nomological network.

Step 1: Identification: Factor Structure of SMIPC

Identifying a proper structure for the SMIPC construct is necessary since it comprises scales from mature and validated instruments in addition to a newly developed item based on prior literature. As suggested by prior literature [e.g., 8], exploratory factor analysis (EFA) of the various factors of SMIPC was conducted followed by confirmatory factor analysis (CFA).

Two sets of EFA were conducted with IBM SPSS software using Principal Components Analysis technique with VARIMAX rotation and Kaiser Normalization. The first EFA included only the four dimensions of CFIP posited by Smith et al. [3]. As shown in Table 1, three components were revealed and all the items loaded cleanly on their respective constructs with no cross loadings. The second EFA included the newly developed scale, privacy policy transparency, in addition to the four dimensions of CFIP posited by Smith et al. [3]. As shown in Table 1, three components were also revealed with the newly developed scale (privacy policy transparency) and two of the dimensions from prior research (unauthorized access and secondary use) converging on the same factor component.

Cronbach Alpha was used to assess the reliability of the factors revealed from the EFAs [17]. Cronbach Alpha for the three factors in both EFAs exceed the 0.70 threshold recommended by Nunnally [18], indicating convergent validity. Since the privacy policy transparency construct loads on the same factor as the composite construct that comprise secondary use and unauthorized access constructs, it is plausible to propose two factor structures for SMIPC. The first SMIPC structure (SMIPC Structure I) can be divided into three dimensions (unauthorized access and secondary use, collection, and error) and the second structure (SMIPC Structure II) into three dimensions (privacy policy transparency, collection, and error).

Table 1. Principal Component Analysis using VARIMAX Rotation

Factor	Items	Component I			
		1	2	3	CA
Collection	COL1		.783		0.82
	COL2		.747		
	COL3		.809		
	COL4		.740		
Error	ERR1			.852	0.92
	ERR2			.812	
	ERR3			.873	
Information Access = Unauthorized Access + Secondary Use of Personal Information	UAC1	.743			0.93
	UAC2	.766			
	UAC3	.819			
	UAC4	.660			
	SUS1	.805			
	SUS2	.765			
	SUS3	.805			
Rotation Sums of Squared Loadings	Total	4.655	2.894	2.720	
	% Variance	33.251	20.671	19.426	
	Cumulative Variance	33.251	53.921	73.347	

CA-Cronbach's Alpha.

Consistent with prior study [3], CFA is used to assess the efficacy of the model structure suggested from the EFA, which contains 14 items. This research follows the procedures used by Stewart and Segars [6] to conduct CFA, which compared covariance matrices based on observed data and the hypothesized models. In the case of this research there are two observed covariance is a 14 × 14 matrix of the measures adopted to measure SMIPC. According to Stewart and Segars [6], CFA allows a researcher to specify, estimate, and re-specify multiple and interrelated dependence relationships as well as unobserved constructs. CFA assesses a hypothesized model by comparing its observed covariance matrix with the implied covariance matrix. The implied matrix is a set of covariances (14 × 14) generated through maximum likelihood estimation as a result of the specified model [6]. The closer the two models are, the better the model fit indicating that the specified model is indicative of the data collected. Goodness-of-fit indices are then used to report the result of the comparison between the observed and implied matrices. In accordance with prior studies [19, 20], multiple fit indices were used for assessing the fit between the observed and implied models in this study. The following section presents four[1] hypothesized models to assess the factorial nature of SMIPC.

Model 1 hypothesizes that all items of SMIPC form into one first-order factor accounting for all the common variance among the 14 items. Prior research [3] measured privacy concern as though it were a unidimensional construct indicating that one first-order factor can be used to explain the underlying data structure. If this model is accepted, then it is appropriate to consider SMIPC as a single dimension that governs similarities in variation among all 14 items.

Model 2 hypothesizes that all 14 items of SMIPC form into two first-order factors: secondary use and unauthorized access is loaded onto one factor and error and collection are loaded onto the second factor. This model proposes that individuals' concern for information privacy on social media sites is divided into two areas: 1) individuals' concern for privacy may be triggered by their perception of other people's access to their personal information and misuse of such information, and 2) users' concern as a result of erroneous collection of personal information on social media sites.

Model 3 hypothesizes that three first-order factors account for the covariance among the 14 items as unauthorized access and secondary use, collection, and error. This model suggests scaling SMIPC as an average of the subscale scores to calculate an overall score. As noted by Stewart and Segars [6], the assumption of this model is that all the items are equally important in computing each factor and each factor is equally vital to computing the overall score for the SMIPC construct.

Model 4 hypothesizes that all items form into three first-order factors, which are then measured by a second-order factor SMIPC. According to Stewart and Segars [6], in such a model, "the inter-correlations among first-

[1] Although only four models are discussed in this article, the four-structure CFIP model proposed in prior research was specified and tested with data collected in this study. The fit indices for the models with four independent measures were not as strong as the 3-factor structure revealed in the context of social media.

order factors form a system of interdependence (or covariation) that is itself important in measuring the construct. Conceptually, each factor and the second-order factor are necessary in capturing the nature of the construct domain [6, p.39]." SMIPC can therefore be defined as three distinct factors as well as the structure of interrelationships among these factors.

Table 2 presents the results of testing all four models for SMIPC. As in prior research [6, 9], fit indices are examined in terms of NFI, GFI, AGFI, CFI, NNFI, Std. RMR, and RMSEA. As shown in the results, Model 1 and Model 2 have poor goodness of fit indices. Models 3 and 4 have acceptable goodness fit indices, but Model 4 (2nd-order factor) indicates better fit to the data.

This result supports Stewart and Segar's [6] thesis that information privacy concern models are better structured as a higher order factor models rather than 1st-order factor models.

Since Model 3 and Model 4 exhibit stronger measures of fit compared to other alternative models, the convergent and discriminant validity of both models are further examined.

Table 2. Measures of Model Fit: Confirmatory Factor Analysis Results for Alternative Factor Structures

Fit Indices	Recommended Indices	Alternative SMIPC Factor Structures			
		Model 1: One 1st-Order Factor	Model 2: Two 1st-Order Factors	Model 3: Three 1st-Order Factors	Model 4: 2nd-Order Factor
χ2		387.70*	306.58*	114.35*	82.65
df		64	63	69	64
χ2/(df)	< 3.00	6.06	4.87	1.66	1.29
NFI	> 0.90	0.87	0.90	0.98	0.97
GFI	> 0.90	0.84	0.85	0.95	0.96
AGFI	> 0.80	0.73	0.75	0.92	0.94
CFI	> 0.90	0.89	0.92	0.98	0.99
NNFI	> 0.90	0.84	0.88	0.98	0.99
Std.RMR	< 0.05	0.08	0.07	0.03	0.03
RMSEA	< 0.06	0.13	0.11	0.05	0.03

*p<0.05; Std. RMR-Standardized RMR.

Table 3. Convergent Validity for Model 3 and Model 4

Construct	Item	Model 3				Model 4			
		Std. Loading	t-value	AVE	CR	Std. Loading	t-value	AVE	CR
Collection	COL1	0.90	8.26	0.76	0.93	0.97	7.79	0.95	0.99
	COL2	0.84	7.43			0.95	7.74		
	COL3	0.94	10.78			0.99	9.44		
	COL4	0.81	7.44			0.99	8.37		
Error	ERR1	0.97	16.24	0.86	0.95	0.89	15.89	0.90	0.96
	ERR2	0.91	15.92			0.99	16.14		
	ERR3	0.90	16.03			0.95	16.66		
Information Access and Use = Unauthorized Access + Secondary Use of Personal Information	UAC1	0.88	16.66	0.87	0.98				
	UAC2	0.99	20.48						
	UAC3	0.98	16.89						
	UAC4	0.94	17.00						
	SUS1	0.90	16.65						
	SUS2	0.90	15.89						
	SUS3	0.92	17.53						

AVE—Average Variance Extracted; CR—Composite Reliability.

As shown in Table 3 the t-values for all the construct items indicate significant factor loadings and provide evidence to support the convergent validity of the items measured [21]. The composite reliability results, shown in Table 3, measure internal consistency of the scales, each exceeding the recommended 0.70 threshold [22], indicating satisfactory reliability for all the factors. The average variance extracted (AVE) for each scale exceeds the recommended 0.50 threshold [22]. Put together, both models demonstrate strong properties of convergent validity.

Although the psychometric properties of Model 3 and Model 4 are strong and satisfactorily fit the data, Model 4 represents the structure of SMIPC more parsimoniously than Model 3.

To assess the discriminant validity of the SMIPC model, correlations among the latent variables are examined as shown in Table 4. Discriminant validity is assessed if the square root of the AVE is larger than correlation coefficients [22]. The result shows that correlations among the latent variables are less than the square root of the AVEs along the diagonals of Table 4. Hence, the measurement model is shown to exhibit strong discriminant validity.

Table 4. Correlations among Latent Variables

	IAC	COL	ERR
Information Access (IAC)	0.96		
Collection (COL)	0.58	0.97	
Error (ERR)	0.68	0.44	0.95

Step 2: Validation: SMIPC within a Nomological Network

Consistent with prior work [6], the construct for SMIPC is tested for nomological validity. In accordance with the approach recommended by Chin [23], establishing the efficacy of a second-order model involves its assessment with other constructs within a nomological network. In accordance to the procedure established by Stewart and Segars [6], a second-order factor is expected to act as a significant mediator when embedded within a network of predictor and consequent variables. Accordingly, SMIPC is placed between a predictor variable (computer anxiety) and a consequent variable (behavioral intention). Stewart and Segars [6] validated CFIP as a mediator between individuals' frustration with the use of computers (i.e., computer anxiety) and their behavioral intention to use it in future. Individuals that are apprehensive or fearful about current or future use of computers are found to have stronger levels of privacy concerns [3, 6]. As such, this article argues that SMIPC will act as a consequent of computer anxiety. Individuals that are anxious about the use of computers are highly likely to be concerned about how their personal information is collected and used on social media platforms.

As for the predictor variable of SMIPC, individuals with higher levels of privacy concerns are more likely in the future to refuse to disclose their personal information, and refuse to use a technology that demands data collection with online merchants. Prior research provides evidence for a negative relationship between privacy concern and behavioral intention [24]. Therefore, a negative relationship is expected between SMIPC and users' behavioral intentions.

Using previously defined scales for computer anxiety [3] and an adaptation of behavioral intentions [6], the analysis of SMIPC is expanded using a 20 × 20 covariance matrix consisting of a 14-item SMIPC scale, a 3-item computer anxiety scale, and a 3-item behavioral intentions scale. Table 5 presents the structural model for Model 5 (1st-order factor model) and Model 6 (2nd-order factor model).

Table 5. Measures of Model Fit: SMIPC within a Nomological Network

Fit Indices	Recommended Indices	Model 5: 1st-Order Factor	Model 6: 2nd-Order Factor
$\chi 2$		158.11	105.17
df		145	101
$\chi 2$/(df)	< 3.00	1.10	1.04
NFI	> 0.90	0.95	0.97
GFI	> 0.90	0.95	0.96
AGFI	> 0.80	0.93	0.94
CFI	> 0.90	0.99	0.99
NNFI	> 0.90	0.99	0.99
Std.RMR	< 0.05	0.04	0.04
RMSEA	<0.06	0.02	0.01

Following recommendations from prior research, fit indices in terms of Normed χ^2, NFI, GFI, AGFI, CFI, NNFI, and RMSEA indicate good model fit for Model 5 and Model 6. Based on the NFI, GFI, AGFI, and RMSEA indices,

Model 6[1] demonstrates stronger fit compared to Model 5. Figure 1 demonstrates both models (Model 5 and Model 6) and associated estimates of SMIPC mediating the relationship between computer anxiety and behavioral intentions. The paths are all significant and consistent with the theoretical prediction. When compared to Model 4 (1st-order factor model), Model 6 (2nd-order factor model) appears to have a better fit.

Discussion and Conclusion

The research program through which this study was conducted seeks to respond to the call [1, 4] for a better understanding of information privacy concerns with interpersonal social interactions in the context of social media. As noted in the call [1], information privacy on social media platforms needs to be conceptualized as a multi-agent phenomenon that involves the volunteer of personal information from individuals to a group or collective under the assumption that shared information will be kept confidential among agents, including social ties members, social media platforms, and third party vendors [1].

It is plausible to expect that privacy issues in the context of social media will become important as consumers' personal information is more readily accessible by other users, vendors, and social media platforms. Although research in the area of information privacy is matured and extensive, the social media context of information privacy research is in its infancy, hence the call for research in this domain [1]. Drawing on Communication Privacy theory [7], this study empirically developed and measured SMIPC based on the three dimensions including, collection of personal information, and errors with the storage and representation of personal information. The three-factor structure of SMIPC was revealed in an exploratory factor analysis (EFA), which was further confirmed through confirmatory factor analysis. Three factors emerged from the EFA with secondary use and unauthorized access loading on one factor, errors loaded on the second factor, and collection loaded on the third factor. Further analysis revealed that the 2nd-order factor model of SMIPC outperformed the 1st-order factor model of SMIPC based on better fit indices.

[1] Discriminant validity was also verified using nested model method recommended by Bagozzi et al. [25], which showed significant differences among all the models, showing that the constructs are distinct from one another. Common method bias analysis was conducted to rule out the variance attributable to the measurement method rather than to the constructs, and none was observed in the data.

The better fit indices for the second-order model of SMIPC does not simply imply that social media users are concerned about these issues, but it also suggest that interdependencies among these issues are vital to measuring individuals' information privacy concerns on social media platforms (SMIPC).

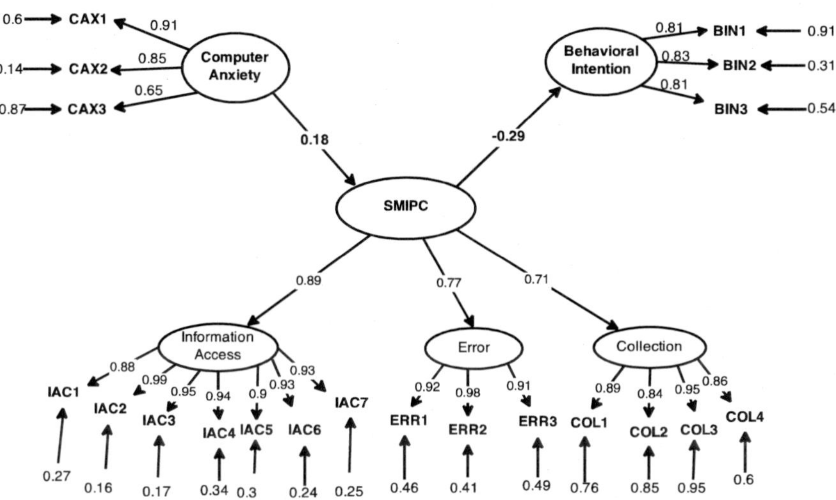

Figure 1. SMIPC as a Second-Order Model within its Nomological Network.

The results of this study provide interesting insights into the dimensionality of SMIPC construct in the context of social interactions. This study therefore contributes to the literature by developing and validating an instrument for measuring individuals' privacy concern on social media platforms. As noted by Stewart and Segars [6], with this validated instrument, further research can now be conducted into the relationships among antecedents and consequences of information privacy concerns on social media platforms. Additionally, researchers are invited to use the instrument developed in this study with confidence due to the strong reliability and validity of the constructs indicated in the results. The SMIPC instrument can now be used as a standardized measure of individuals' concern for information privacy on social media platforms.

Although the results presented are insightful, there are limitations associated with the conduct of this study. As noted in prior research [6, p.45], results of confirmatory factor analysis must be interpreted cautiously, since the "criteria for comparing [competing] models and assessing goodness-of-fit indices are relative and not absolute." This suggests that a model is a good representation of reality when it can be replicated in subsequent studies. As such, researchers the authors call on researchers to further confirm the validity of SMIPC in other contexts.

CONTRIBUTION

Drawing on CPM theory, this study seeks to define the nature of privacy concerns in the social media context based on three boundary coordination rules [7], including (a) information access (rooted in linkage and permeability coordination rules), (b) error in storing and representation of personal information (rooted in ownership coordination rule), and (c) collection of personal information (rooted in permeability coordination rule). In the social media context, this article argues that users are likely to become concerned about the safety of their personal information shared on social media platforms with the knowledge that other users, the platform, and third party vendors may gain access to their personal information and misappropriate it. In particular, social media users' concern over information access and information misuse can be triggered by the violation of linkage and permeability rules i.e., when linkage to personal data occurs and vendors have access to users' personal information without expressed consent from the user. With regards to error, users' perception of error can become salient with the violation of ownership rules i.e., when vendors and social media platforms are able to make decisions about the possession of users' personal information. Finally, users' perception of collection of their personal information can become salient when permeability rules are violated i.e., when social media platforms and their vendors can readily access users' personal information without consent. Table 6 presents a summary of information privacy measurement instruments with their theoretical foundations.

APPENDIX: CONCERN FOR INFORMATION PRIVACY MEASUREMENT SCALES

Computer Anxiety (CAX) [Source: [6]]

1. I am sometimes frustrated by increasing automation in my home
2. I am sometimes afraid that I will delete all my important files

3. I am sometimes afraid that I will mistakenly send personal information to the wrong recipient

Concern for Information Privacy [Source: [3]]

Collection (COL)

1. It usually bothers me when social media sites ask me for personal information
2. It usually bothers me when companies ask me to like or follow their social media sites during transactions
3. It bothers me to give personal information to so many people on the social media sites I am registered with
4. I am concerned that companies are collecting too much personal information about me through the social media sites I am registered on

Unauthorized Access (UAC)

1. Computer databases that contain personal information should be protected from unauthorized access—no matter how much it costs
2. Social media sites should take more steps to make sure that unauthorized people cannot access personal information in their computers
3. Databases that contain personal information should be stored in a highly secured location
4. Social media sites should delete a user's account for illegally accessing other users' personal information

Errors (ERR)

1. Companies should take more steps to make sure that personal information in their files is accurate
2. Companies should have better procedures to correct errors in personal information
3. Companies should devote more time and effort to verifying the accuracy of the personal information in their databases

Secondary Use (SUS)

1. Social media sites and companies should not use personal information for any purpose unless it has been authorized by the individuals who provide the information

2. When people give personal information to a social media site or company for some reason, the company should never use the information for any other purpose
3. Social media sites or companies should never share personal information with other companies unless it has been authorized but the individual who provided the information

Behavioral Intentions (BIN) [Source: [6]]
How likely are you, within the next three years to…
1. Create an online account with an organization or company to complete a transaction?
2. Create an online account with an organization or company you frequently do business with?
3. Register online with a company or organization that you frequently do business with?

REFERENCES

[1] Xu, H., and BéLanger, F., "Information Systems Journal Special Issue on: Reframing Privacy in a Networked World," *Information Systems Journal* (23, 2013, 371-375.

[2] Bélanger, F., and Crossler, R.E., "Privacy in the digital age: a review of information privacy research in information systems," *MIS Quarterly* (35:4), 2011, 1017-1042.

[3] Smith, H.J., Milberg, S.J., and Burke, S.J., "Information privacy: measuring individuals' concerns about organizational practices," *MIS Quarterly*, 1996, 167-196.

[4] Lipford, R.H., Wisniewski, J.P., Lampe, C., Kisselburgh, L., and Caine, K., "Workshop on Reconciling Privacy with Social Media", The ACM Conference on Computer Supported Cooperative Work, 2012

[5] Aral, S., Dellarocas, C., and Godes, D., "Introduction to the Special Issue-Social Media and Business Transformation: A Framework for Research," *Information Systems Research* (24:1), 2013, 3-13.

[6] Stewart, K.A., and Segars, A.H., "An empirical examination of the concern for information privacy instrument," *INFORMATION SYSTEMS RESEARCH* (13:1), 2002, 36-49.

[7] Petronio, S., Boundaries of privacy: Dialectics of disclosure, State University of New York Press, New York, 2002.

[8] Malhotra, N.K., Kim, S.S., and Agarwal, J., "Internet users' information privacy concerns (IUIPC): the construct, the scale, and a causal model," *Information Systems Research* (15:4), 2004, 336-355.

[9] Xu, H., Gupta, S., Rosson, M.B., and Carroll, J.M., "Measuring Mobile Users' Concerns for Information Privacy", Proceedings of 33rd Annual International Conference on Information Systems (ICIS 2012), 2012

[10] Epic, "Pressure Mounts on Facebook to Withdraw Proposed Changes, New Scrutiny of "Faceprints"", in (Editor, 'ed.'^'eds.'): Book Pressure Mounts on Facebook to Withdraw Proposed Changes, New Scrutiny of "Faceprints", Electronic Privacy Information Center, 2013

[11] Jin, S.-a.A., ",ÄúTo disclose or not to disclose, that is the question,Äù: A structural equation modeling approach to communication privacy management in e-health," *Computers in Human Behavior* (28:1), 2012, 69-77.

[12] Petronio, S., "Communication privacy management theory: What do we know about family privacy regulation?," *Journal of Family Theory & Review* (2:3), 2010, 175-196.

[13] Child, J.T., Pearson, J.C., and Petronio, S., "Blogging, communication, and privacy management: Development of the blogging privacy management measure," *Journal of the American Society for Information Science and Technology* (60:10), 2009, 2079-2094.

[14] Dwyer, C., Hiltz, S., and Passerini, K., "Trust and Privacy: A Comparison of Facebook and MySpace," *Americas Conference on Information Systems*, 2007,

[15] Son, J.-Y., and Kim, S.S., "Internet users' information privacy-protective responses: A taxonomy and a nomological model," *MIS Quarterly* (32:3), 2008, 503-529.

[16] Smith, A., Raine, L., and Zickuhr, K., "College students and technology", in (Editor, 'ed.'^'eds.'): *Book College students and technology,* Pew Research Center, Washington, D.C. (July 19, 2011), 2011

[17] Bagozzi, R.P., Casual Methods in Marketing, John Wiley and Sons, New York, 1980.

[18] Nunnally, J., "*Psychometric Theory*", McGraw-Hill, New York, NY, 1978

[19] Bentler, P.M., and Bonett, D.G., "Significance tests and goodness of fit in the analysis of covariance structures," *Psychological Bulletin* (88:3), 1980, 588.

[20] Marsh, H.W., and Hocevar, D., "A new, more powerful approach to multitrait-multimethod analyses: Application of second-order confirmatory factor analysis," *Journal of Applied Psychology* (73:1), 1988, 107.

[21] Anderson, J.C., and Gerbing, D.W., "Structural Equation Modeling in Practice: A Review and Recommendation Two-Step Approach," *Psychological Bulletin* (103:3), 1988, 411-423.

[22] Fornell, C., and Larcker, D.F., "Evaluating structural equation models with unobservable variables and measurement error," *Journal of Marketing Research*, 1981, 39-50.

[23] Chin, W.W., "Issues and Opinion on Structural Equation Modeling," *MIS Quarterly* (22:1), 1998, VII-XVI.

[24] Xu, H., and Teo, H.-H., "Alleviating Consumers' Privacy Concerns in Location-Based Services: A Psychological Control Perspective", Proceedings of the Twenty-Fifth Annual International Conference on Information Systems (ICIS 2004), 2004, pp. 793-806.

[25] Bagozzi, R.P., Yi, Y., and Phillips, L.W., "Assessing construct validity in organizational research," *Administrative Science Quarterly* (36:3), 1991.

[26] Podsakoff, P.M., Mackenzie, S.B., Lee, J.-Y., and Podsakoff, N.P., "Common method biases in behavioral research: a critical review of the literature and recommended remedies," *Journal of Applied Psychology* (88:5), 2003, 879.

[27] Bansal, G., Zahedi, F., and Gefen, D., "The moderating influence of privacy concern on the efficacy of privacy assurance mechanisms for building trust: A multiple-context investigation", *Proceedings of 29th Annual International Conference on Information Systems* (ICIS 2008), 2008.

[28] http://www.ftc.gov/reports/privacy2000/privacy2000.pdf, accessed April 20, 2014.

[29] Loeffler, C., "Privacy issues in social media," *IP Litigator*, 2012, 12-18.

[30] Preibusch, S., Hoser, B., Gürses, S., and Berendt, B., "Ubiquitous social networks – opportunities and challenges for privacy-aware user modelling", in (Editor, 'ed.'^'eds.'): Book Ubiquitous social networks – opportunities and challenges for privacy-aware user modelling, 2007.

In: Social Media
Editor: Annmarie Bennet

ISBN: 978-1-63463-175-4
© 2015 Nova Science Publishers, Inc.

Chapter 2

FEAR OR DANGER THREAT MESSAGING: THE DARK SIDE OF SOCIAL MEDIA

Fay Cobb Payton and Cherie Conley
North Carolina State University, North Carolina, US

ABSTRACT

Social media is said to be one way to disseminate health information. With the proliferation of social media tools, such as Facebook, Twitter, Tumblr, and YouTube, more millennials are engaged in health information seeking and discovery.

To develop targeted health messages to this demographic, web-based applications and social media tools informed by millennials' perceptions can be effective. Prior research has shown that social media can be effective in dampening the stigma associated with health conditions, such as HIV, even in cases where consumers simply engage in health information seeking behaviors.

We use the Extended Parallel Process Model (EPPM) of behavior change communication to examine specifically how Black college-aged and matriculating women perceive the threat of HIV and their ability to prevent transmission.

The purpose of this study is to assess perceived threat and perceived efficacy via the EPPM in order to inform the ongoing social media development of HIV prevention messages for myHealthImpact Network.org, an online experience targeting Black women.

A convenience sample of 49 Black women was recruited and invited to complete both paper and pencil, and online surveys. Overall, the sample had positive EPPM scores, meaning that the participants perceived HIV as a severe threat to which they feel mildly susceptible, but very capable of preventing.

The sample respondents' positive EPPM scores indicate that messages targeting this group should continue to stress the severity of HIV and their susceptibility to the disease as well as strategies to prevent its transmission. Thus, tailored fear appeals can offer an effective messaging approach to communicating the threat of HIV to this population. These results offer insights into how social media can be used, consumed and perceived among diverse populations.

INTRODUCTION

In the United States, Black women share a disproportionate burden of HIV/AIDS [2, 7]. The rate of HIV diagnoses for Black women is 20 times the rate for White women [7]. Young Black women living in the South are the most impacted by the disease [2].

Prior studies have shown that interventions aimed at preventing HIV among low income Black women, those with substance abuse conditions, and Black youth, had some long-term success [14, 20]. Few studies, however, have addressed HIV risk among college-educated and matriculating Black women [10, 16]. College students, in general, are more susceptible to HIV due to increased risk taking in undergraduate years of matriculation [1, 2], specifically as it relates to the use of drugs and alcohol as well as engaging in unsafe sexual practices [1, 11].

Black women may be particularly vulnerable to HIV for several reasons. First, with fewer Black men on college campuses than Black women [3], "man sharing" and adherence to sexual preferences of male partners results in a higher risk for HIV infection [7, 10]. This is especially important given that Black men are less likely than men from other racial groups to identify as being homosexual, while engaging in sexual relationships with both women and men.

The purpose of this study is to use the Extended Parallel Process Model (EPPM) to better understand perceptions of HIV threat and efficacy to help determine the types of social media messages needed to increase HIV awareness among college-educated and matriculating Black women.

Background

EPPM

Multiple studies have assessed and attempted to address the factors that may influence health behaviors. Interventions shown to be the most effective are based on established behavior change theories [13]. One such theory is the Extended Parallel Process Model (EPPM) which is a behavior change communication strategy that utilizes fear appeals, when necessary, to encourage behavior change [24]. In the 1980s, when HIV first became a public health issue and little was known about the disease, prevention and public awareness campaigns often relied on fear appeals - messages designed to frighten people into making better lifestyle choices to elicit behavior change [19]. Fear appeals can show pictures or describe scenarios in graphic or even gruesome details about what may happen as a consequence of not heeding the advice presented in the messages. As more information has been learned about the disease process and medical technology has produced accessible treatment options, fear appeals have been used less frequently.

Conversely, the relatively high rates of HIV among Black women, especially in the context of high rates of testing and level of knowledge, and the fact that fear appeals are often more effective among youth as opposed to adults [9], raises the question whether or not fear appeals can again be of use to address this health issue. The EPPM [8, 24] assesses perceived susceptibility and seriousness of a health condition, collectively conceptualized as ‘threat’, as well as perceived efficacy in avoiding that particular health condition. According to the framework, there are two response pathways that individuals or groups can have when confronted with a threat, such as HIV. These two response pathways are either ‘Fear’ or ‘Danger’. When creating social media prevention messages, it is important to know which response pathway characterizes the priority population because depending on the pathway, certain types of messages are recommended for maximum effectiveness.

EPPM: Fear and Danger Messaging

When individuals see HIV as a threat, but score *low* on the efficacy scale, they have a ‘Fear’ response. The fear response reflects an internal emotion that leads those individuals to reject messages that focus on increasing awareness of the disease threat because they are already aware of and afraid of the threat. Instead of developing messages that heighten their fear of the disease, it would be more valuable to develop HIV prevention messages that clearly define and emphasize ways to prevent the disease [24]. It would be most important to clearly explain the specific methods to avoid transmission and to present them in a way that makes it clear that these methods will be effective. They should also boost the audience's confidence that they can perform the suggested action. For example, messages to increase efficacy might provide statistics that show just how effective the methods are to avoid HIV. They may also present individuals who appear to be in the priority audience modeling desired behavior, such as negotiation skills in sexual decision making or correct condom use. Role-play is also encouraged [22].

On the other hand, when individuals see HIV as a threat, but score *high* on the efficacy scale, it indicates that while they feel that the disease is severe and that they may be susceptible to it, they are fully capable of preventing infection. This is the 'Danger' response and individuals who are in this category would respond most positively to messages that reiterate the threat of HIV as well as prevention methods [24]. Messages can be very straightforward and possibly disturbing. The fearful situation that is displayed in the message, however, must reflect the specific fears and interests of the priority audience. For instance, an HIV awareness message aiming to improve awareness among youth might show the social isolation of a young person diagnosed with HIV because that is one of the biggest fears of youth. It is essential that the messages also show ways to prevent HIV to address efficacy. Both fear and efficacy components should be featured equally in social media and other forms of messaging [22]. Since being introduced by Witte in 1992, the EPPM has been used in several studies to address a variety of health issues [6]. However, there has been limited, if any, use of the EPPM to explore how college-educated and matriculating Black women perceive the threat of HIV as well as their own sense of efficacy in preventing the transmission of the disease.

Impacts of Social Media

Among young adults specifically, a recent study [22] showed that 62% get all of their news online, and 75% use social media sites daily. Further, there is widespread use of cellular phones and other mobile devices, computers, web based technologies, and social media for accessing and disseminating health information [12]. While a higher percentage of Whites than Blacks use the web, Black college students access the internet at about the same rates of White college students. Further, Black youth are slightly more likely than their White counterparts (96% vs. 90%) to use social media sites and Twitter, in particular [21]. Yet, it has been discovered that some organizations and individuals online engage in anti-social, flaring and narcissistic behaviors. This is considered the dark side of social media [4]. Thus, although there seems to be buy-in and enthusiastic use of the internet and social media for information exchange, in order for that to continue or improve, there is certainly a need to continue to build trust among members of certain groups who may already be marginalized because of their medical conditions, race, religion or any other intersectional characteristics [11].

While information and communication technology (ICT) has not yet been the magic bullet to curb all health disparities, ICT is a promising tool in the field of health behavior change [18]. Studies have shown that people suffering from stigmatized conditions often delay visiting health care workers for fear of judgment, feelings of guilt or shame, and outright discrimination [5]. The internet, however, may be a place where people can disconnect themselves from the stigma of their disease and, with some anonymity, engage in penalty-free health information seeking. In fact, this is exactly what researchers found when they conducted a study which compared the online health-information seeking behaviors of two groups- those with chronic conditions and those with stigmatized illnesses, such as depression and HIV. Those with stigmatized conditions were found not only to be more likely than the chronic condition group to use the internet to seek out information, but also were more likely to seek follow-up treatment or care afterwards [5].

For instance, Payton, et al. [17] conducted focus groups of Black female college students between 18 and 24 years old. These sessions concentrated on online health information seeking and HIV messaging imparted by existing ICT platforms to discern the participants' perceptions of cultural identity, language and spirit (e.g., technology designers, medical jargon). This research resulted in the creation of the myHealthImpactNetwork.org experience. MyHealthImpactNetwork.org was developed initially to motivate healthy sexual behavior choices, and increase knowledge and awareness of HIV among Black women, especially those young and college matriculating.

Though the MyHealthImpactNetwork.org platform had already been developed by the timing of this study, herein, and is currently being utilized with a growing following of users, there remains a need to reassess the priority audience's perceptions of HIV in order to evaluate current social media prevention messages and implement strategies to better address users' needs. To this end, the assessment of the prevention messages is critical as the myHealthImpactNetwork.org team uses an iterative design methodology to continuously improve the user experience for its target group.

Due to multiple factors that increase Black women's susceptibility to HIV, there is a need for targeted health behavior change campaigns to address HIV prevention among this group. The purpose of this study is to use the EPPM framework to assess perceptions of threat and efficacy. This enables an evaluation of the potential social media effectiveness of MyHealthImpact Network.org, and can suggest revisions to the website messaging strategy based on the following results.

METHODS

Sample and Research Design

Participants were recruited onsite from one historically Black college and university (HBCU) and one a predominantly White institution (PWI). Onsite recruitment was done at a university community health fair, a community festival, and health information forum. Informational booths and a short presentation about @myHealthImpactNetwork were provided to potential participants at these events. Each event where participants were recruited involved Black college-educated or matriculating students, particularly women. Participants also were recruited online through the myHealthImpactNetwork.org website. After receiving institutional review board (IRB) approval, recruitment took place from March 2013 to April 2013.

Procedure

Online and onsite recruitment scripts were developed and approved by the IRB and presented to potential participants. After agreeing to volunteer, participants were presented with a consent form to sign. The consent form mentioned the purpose of the study, explained that it was both anonymous and confidential, and that participation was voluntary and could be stopped at any time. Onsite respondents were asked to complete the survey privately. Each completed survey was placed into a sealed box. Volunteers who agreed to take the survey online were emailed a website URL which featured the survey link.

Online respondents' survey answers were immediately loaded into a data storage file. Upon completion of the survey, as roughly verified by a check of completed surveys by the second author, onsite respondents were given the opportunity to win a $10 gift certificate as an incentive for completion by completing raffle tickets. Online participants were not asked to provide contact information, and therefore were not included in the incentive due to the inability to contact them after survey completion. Recruitment efforts resulted in an initial convenience sample of 56 women, self-identifying as Black, who completed the survey. Seven of the surveys were removed due to incompletion (i.e., blank items) - thus, leaving a total of 49 participants for the sample. The term 'Black' is used to describe the women in the study who self-identify as African-American, Caribbean, African or multiethnic Black.

Information on demographic characteristics, including age, relationship status, educational level, and income, was also collected to ensure that the sample population surveyed represented the study's priority group. Table 1 shows the demographic characteristics of the participants. Ages ranged from 19 to over 36. All of the women were either enrolled in college or had graduated at the time of the study. Most of the women (71%) reported that they were not currently in a relationship.

Research Questionnaire

We used Witte's EPPM, a validated survey instrument, to assess perceptions of HIV threat as well as efficacy within the sample population. The survey has twelve items: six to assess perceptions of disease threat, as measured by perceptions of disease severity and personal susceptibility, and six items to assess efficacy, as measured by perceived self-efficacy and response efficacy. Table 2 includes the survey items [24].

Threat Measures – Susceptibility and Severity

The first six items of the survey scale assess respondents' perceptions of HIV threat - three examine perceptions of severity of the illness itself and three focus on personal susceptibility to contracting HIV. Each response is scored from 1(low) to 5 (high) via a Likert scale. Scores for all six questions are added to provide one score for the threat scale.

For this study, individual participants' scores for each question are averaged to provide a single total representing the entire sample as shown in Table 2.

Efficacy Measures – Self and Response

The last six items on the survey assess efficacy, which has two subcategories – response efficacy and self-efficacy. Questions for the response efficacy portion of the scale focus on how much a respondent feels that there are reliable tools (e.g., condoms) available to help prevent the condition,which in this case is HIV.

The self-efficacy subcategory is captured by a respondent's perceptions about her own ability to access and use those tools. As with the threat scale, each response is scored from 1 (strongly disagree) to 5 (strongly agree), and individual participants' scores for each question are averaged to provide a single total that is shown in Table 2.

Critical Values

The critical value is obtained by subtracting the sum of the values for the six threat items from the sum of the values for the six efficacy items. A positive critical value indicates a 'danger' response while a negative critical value indicates a 'fear' response [8].

Data Analysis

Data were entered into an Excel spreadsheet and imported in SAS for data analysis. Descriptive statistics were used to summarize demographic data. Responses to perceptions of HIV severity and personal susceptibility as well as efficacy were examined in aggregate.

RESULTS

Response Pathway of Sample Respondents

The EPPM survey instrument assesses respondents' perceptions of threat and efficacy and yields a critical value based on their responses. The respondents in this study scored positively when asked about both perceptions of the threat of HIV (average = 3.3, sum = 19.8), and efficacy (average = 4.2, sum =25.1). The sum scores of the two categories yielded a positive critical value score of +5.2 for the entire sample. The positive critical value indicates that the sample can be classified as having a 'Danger' (as opposed to 'Fear') response to HIV and is suggestive of the types of potentially effective social media messages that would be associated with a 'Danger' response.

Table 1. Demographics of Study Population and Mean EPPM Scores Stratified by Demographic Characteristics

		Demographic characteristics of the respondents (N =49)			
N	%		Mean (S.D.)	F score	p value
		Age			
32	65%	19-25	5.2 (7.12)		
13	27%	26-35	5.6 (3.64)	0.32	0.731
4	8%	35<	7.8 (3.59)		
		Education Completed			
29	59%	Some college	5.6 (6.12)	1.74	0.159
10	20%	Completed college	3.5(8.02)		
4	8%	Some graduate school	9 (4.08)		
6	12%	Completed graduate school	9 (0.89)		
		Relationship Status			
1	2%	Married	8 (-)	0.63	0.607
7	14%	Long term	6.9 (4.06)		
6	12%	New relationship	7.8 (3.19)		
35	71%	Not currently in a relationship	4.7(6.79)		
		Personal Income			
28	57%	$<15,000	5.8(6.39)	0.64	0.636
5	10%	$15000-24,999	6.2(2.95)		
4	8%	$25,000-34,999	2.25(12.23)		
5	10%	$35,000-49,999	3(3.46)		
7	14%	$50,000 and above	7.1(3.02)		

Table 2. EPPM Scores: Threat and Efficacy Scores

<table>
<tr><td colspan="2">Threat Scale</td><td>Average Survey response (Strongly disagree=1 Strongly agree=5)</td><td colspan="2">Efficacy Scale</td><td>Average Survey Response (Strongly disagree=1 Strongly agree=5)</td></tr>
<tr><td rowspan="3">SEVERITY Measures</td><td>I believe that HIV/AIDS infection is severe</td><td>4.9</td><td rowspan="3">SELF-EFFICACY Measures</td><td>I am able to wear condoms to prevent getting HIV/AIDS</td><td>4.4</td></tr>
<tr><td>I believe that HIV/AIDS infection has serious negative consequences</td><td>4.8</td><td>Wearing condoms is easy to do to prevent getting HIV/AIDS</td><td>4.2</td></tr>
<tr><td>I believe that HIV/AIDS infection is extremely harmful</td><td>4.8</td><td>Wearing condoms to prevent HIV/AIDS is convenient</td><td>4.1</td></tr>
<tr><td colspan="2">Threat Scale</td><td>Average Survey response (Strongly disagree=1 Strongly agree=5)</td><td colspan="2">Efficacy Scale</td><td>Average Survey Response (Strongly disagree=1 Strongly agree=5)</td></tr>
<tr><td rowspan="3">SUSCEPTIBILITY Measures</td><td>I am at risk for getting HIV/AIDS</td><td>2.0</td><td rowspan="3">RESPONSE EFFICACY Measures</td><td>Using condoms works in preventing HIV/AIDS</td><td>4.0</td></tr>
<tr><td>It is likely that I will contract HIV/AIDS.</td><td>1.5</td><td>Using condoms is effective in preventing HIV/AIDS</td><td>4.0</td></tr>
<tr><td>It is possible that I will contract HIV/AIDS.</td><td>1.9</td><td>If I use condoms, I am less likely to get HIV/AIDS</td><td>4.4</td></tr>
<tr><td colspan="2">Threat Response Average:</td><td>3.3</td><td colspan="2">Efficacy Response Average:</td><td>4.2</td></tr>
<tr><td colspan="2">Threat Response Sum:</td><td>19.8</td><td colspan="2">Efficacy Response Sum:</td><td>25.1</td></tr>
<tr><td colspan="6">Critical Value for Sample Population (Σ Efficacy - Σ Threat) =+5.2</td></tr>
</table>

Comparing the respondents' average score for the two HIV threat measures and two HIV efficacy measures illustrates the perceptions of the priority population more specifically. According to Witte and Cho [8], mean scores between 4 and 5 indicate very strong feelings of agreement in the particular category being measured. In this study, the mean scores of participants' perceptions of severity, response efficacy and self-efficacy were all between 4 and 5. Only the susceptibility measure scored low at 1.8.

Discussion

In this study, we used the Extended Parallel Process Model (EPPM) to assess perceptions of HIV threat and efficacy to help guide the development and revision of HIV prevention messages for myHealthImpactNetwork.org, an online health awareness platform, targeting college-aged and matriculating Black women. The positive EPPM critical value score of the sample group illustrates that the respondents perceive HIV as a threat and also feel that they have the tools necessary to combat the disease. Hence, the study's results inform the development of social media messages to create the @myHealth ImpactNetwork experience.

Low Feelings of Susceptibility

Results of the study were consistent with previous studies focusing on Black women who showed high levels of awareness of HIV and belief of the severity of the disease, while also having low feelings of susceptibility. Using Witte's model, results also show a high level of self-efficacy and response efficacy, indicating that this particular group is aware of how to prevent HIV transmission and feels very confident in their ability to do so. While this study did not aim to research reasons why susceptibility beliefs are low among this group, it is possible that strong feelings of efficacy may mitigate some of the perceptions of personal susceptibility and should be taken into account when designing social media messages.

In an effort to better inform the priority audience, we are aware that the dark side of social media and vigilant messaging must be taken into account. The threat and efficacy social media messages should not assume that one is infected with the stigmatized condition, particularly when the experience is messaging prevention and awareness. Further, social media messaging should not include judgmental or stereotypical tendencies as Black women are not a monolithic group. As pointed out in Payton and Kvasny (under review), "*…this is the stigma of being publicly associated with and participating in the HIV prevention discourse. The participants offered insights about digital participation and the negative assumptions that the broader society, and even some in their own social networks, would have about them personally.*"

Study Limitations

The main limitation of this study is the small sample size. While some patterns may be observed, without a larger sample, results can only tentatively be generalized to the larger population of college-educated and matriculating Black women in the United States. Another limitation in this study is the possibility of selection bias given that about half of respondents were recruited from events with health-related themes. It is possible that the students who chose to attend these events may have perceptions of HIV that are different from the general population. Another possible limitation is social desirability bias. Although surveys were anonymous and confidential, it is possible that participants may have felt social pressure to respond in a manner perceived as socially acceptable as opposed to providing honest answers.

Conclusion

The goal of this study was to better understand perceptions of HIV among college-educated and matriculating Black women, a subpopulation of a group that is disproportionately affected by HIV. The purpose was to better understand this group's perceptions of threat and efficacy in order to create effective HIV prevention social media messages. In order to craft the most accurate messages, there has to be an accurate and thorough understanding of the target audience. The better the audience's perceptions are understood, the better and more specific the social media messages that can be crafted [22]. According to the EPPM, the responses of the sample of women surveyed in this study reflect the EPPM's 'Danger' response (as opposed to the 'Fear' response) pathway with regard to their perceptions of HIV threat and efficacy.

Although the study focused on assessing perceptions of threat and efficacy, and did not look at the possible causes or factors that may contribute to those perceptions, results can still provide some guidance on what types of prevention messages should be promoted to reach the priority audience of college-educated and matriculating Black women. The positive critical value score of the study sample suggests that messages emphasizing *both* threat and efficacy would be most effective. Thus, it is recommended that online platforms and social media outlets, such as MyHealthImpactNetwork.org and others targeting this group, not only continue to share information about the most effective methods of prevention, and boost confidence in individuals' ability to use those methods, but also provide specific information on disease severity and how it affects college-educated and matriculating Black women.

For example, the platform should provide statistics, which refer to the specific risk of college-educated and matriculating Black women. Digital content featuring those affected and infected by HIV would resonate with this younger audience, but it is critical to see images reflective of the same demographic. It is, likewise, important to reduce stereotypes, which were often heard while recruiting participants at their college events. According to Witte [24], "To increase perceived susceptibility to a health threat, messages need to emphasize or illustrate how the health threat occurs to people who are demographically, psychographically, and in any other way possible, identical to your intended audiences or clients." Thus, the messaging recommended to address threat overall, would also be particularly useful in addressing the especially low susceptibility scores of the target population [1, 8]. Future research should include exploration and better understanding of what drives perceptions of low HIV susceptibility among college-educated or matriculating Black women.

REFERENCES

[1] Adefuye, A. S. et. al., (2009). HIV sexual risk behaviors and perception of risk among college students: implications for planning interventions. *BMC Public Health,* 9, 281-294.

[2] Alleyne, B. and Wodarski, J., (2009). Psychosocial factors that contribute to HIV/AIDS Risk behaviors among young Black college women. *Journal of Human Behavior in the Social Environment,* 19(2), 142-158. Retrieved from: http://dx.doi.org/10.1080/10911350802687117

[3] Alleyne, B. and Gaston, G. (2010). Gender disparity and HIV risk among young Black women in college: a literature review. *Journal of Women and Social Work,* 5(2), 135-145.

[4] Basulto, D., (2014). The emerging dark side of social media. The Washington Post. Retrieved from: http://www.washingtonpost.com/blogs/innovations/wp/2014/04/08/the-emerging-dark-side-of-social-networks/

[5] Berger, M., Wagner, T. H. and Baker, L. C. (2005), "Internet use and stigmatized illness", *Social Science and Medicine*, Vol. 61, pp. 1821-1827.

[6] Campo, S., Askelson, N. M., Carter, K. D., and Losch, M., (2012). Segmenting audiences and tailoring messages: using the extended parallel process model and cluster analysis to improve health campaigns. *Social Marketing Quarterly,* 18(2) 98-111.

[7] Centers for Disease Control, National Center for HIV/AIDS, Viral Hepatitis, STD, and TB Prevention, Division of HIV/AIDS Prevention. Fast Facts: HIV Among African-Americans. February 2013.

[8] Cho, H. and Witte, K., (2005). Managing fear in public health campaigns: a theory-based formative evaluation process. *Health Promotion and Practice,* 6(4), 482-490.

[9] Ferguson, G. and Phau, I., (2013). Adolescent and young adult response to fear appeals in anti-smoking messages. *Young Consumers: Insight and Ideas for Responsible Marketers,* 14(2), 155 – 166.

[10] Freeman, C. (2010). The missing element: incorporating culturally-specific clinical practices in HIV prevention programs for African-American females. *Journal of Cultural Diversity,* 17(2), 51-55.

[11] Ho, L. A., Kuo, T. H., and Binshan, L. (2012), "How social identification and trust influence organizational online knowledge sharing", *Internet Research,* Vol. 22, No. 1., pp. 4-28.

[12] Jones, R. and Lacroix, L. J., (2012). Streaming weekly soap opera video episodes to smartphones in a randomized controlled trial to reduce HIV risk in young urban African American/Black women. *AIDS Behavior,* 16, 1341–1358. doi 10.1007/s10461-012-0170-9

[13] Lyles, C. M., Kay, L. S., Crepaz, N., Herbst, J. H., Passin, W. F., Kim, A. S., Mullins, M. M., (2007). Best-evidence interventions: findings from a systematic review of HIV behavioral interventions for us populations at high risk, 2000–2004. *American Journal of Public Health,* 97(1), 133-143.

[14] Nunn, A., (2011). Low perceived risk and high HIV prevalence among a predominantly African American population participating in Philadelphia's rapid HIV testing program. *AIDS Patient Care and STDS,* 25(4), 229-235. doi: 10.1089/apc.2010.0313

[15] O'Leary, A., Goodhart, F., Jemmott, L. S., Boccher-Lattimore, D., (1992). Predictors of safer sex on the college campus: a social cognitive theory analysis. *Journal of American College Health.* 40(6), 254-263.

[16] Painter, J. E. et.al., (2012). College graduation reduces vulnerability to STIs/HIV among African-American young adult women. *Women's Health Issues,* 22(3), e303–e310.

[17] Payton, F. C., Kiwanuka-Tondo, J. and Kvasny, L. (2012). Black Female Voices: Designing an HIV Information Artifact, 4th International Conference on the Applied Human Factors and Ergonomics, Taylor and Francis Group Publisher, San Francisco, CA.

[18] Payton, F. C., (2009). Beyond the IT magic bullet: HIV prevention education and public policy. *Journal of Health Disparities Research and Practice,* 3(2). 13-33.

[19] Perloff, R. M., (2001). Persuading people to have safer sex. Lawrence Earlbaum Associates, Inc: Mahwah, NJ., pp. 75-77.

[20] Romer, D., Sznitman, S., DiClemente, R., Salazar, L. F., Vanable, P. A., Carey, M. P., Hennessy, M., Juzang, I., (2009). Mass media as an HIV-prevention strategy: using culturally sensitive messages to reduce HIV-associated sexual behavior of at-risk African-American youth. *American Journal of Public Health,* 99(12), 2150–2159.

[21] Smith, A., (2014). African-Americans and technology use. *PEW Research Internet Project.* Retrieved from: http://www.pewinternet.org/ 2014/01/06/african- americans-and- technology-use/

[22] Thesenvitz, J. (2000). Fear appeals for tobacco control. Council for a Tobacco Free Ontario, February 2000. Retrieved from: http:// www.thcu.ca/infoandresources.cfm

[23] Vahlberg, V. (2010). Fitting into their Lives: A Survey of three studies about youth media usage. Newspaper Association of America Foundation. Retrieved from: http://www.americanpressinstitute.org/wp-content/uploads/2013/09/NIE_Fitting_into_their_lives.pdf

[24] Witte, K. et al., (1996). Predicting risk behaviors: development and validation of a Diagnostic scale. *Journal of Health Communication: International Perspectives,* 1(4), 317-342.

In: Social Media
Editor: Annmarie Bennet
ISBN: 978-1-63463-175-4
© 2015 Nova Science Publishers, Inc.

Chapter 3

THE USE OF SOCIAL MEDIA FOR JOB PLACEMENT IN CAREER CENTRES OF FOUR EUROPEAN UNIVERSITIES: OPPORTUNITIES AND RISKS

Ginevra Gravili*
University of Salento, Italy
Department of Economics,
Ecotekne, via per Monteroni, Lecce

ABSTRACT

The process of interaction between individuals, through the use of social media, is one of the most complex problems that theorists have had to analyze in recent years (Richards, 2007; Kolbitsch and Maurer, 2006; Kaplan and Haenlein, 2010; etc.).

Social media tools are becoming an important presence in recruitment processes, transforming them.

Today many organizations are facing a challenge: they have to make choices in order to allow their operators to use this new method of communication with their students and with firms or forbid it. The rapid changes that the diffusion of social media has had in the communication processes would undoubtedly impose a drastic change: the use of social media allow an instant sharing of ideas, opinions, knowledge and

* ginevra.gravili@unisalento.it.

experiences, creating a new "space-time" dimension that could be translated in a new way (additional) to "recruit" workers. Although there are a lot of benefits and promises from social media, however several risks are associated with their use. The ambiguity related to legal and ethical issues (for example individual privacy) of social media, at the same time, contains the enthusiasm related to the potentialities that social media offer. In particular this chapter aims at analyzing the perceived risks and benefits of social media in job placement offices of Universities in four countries (Italy, Switzerland, Austria and Germany) and at providing an analysis of the phenomenon of social recruitment in Universities: it will be done through the analysis of the use of this instrument for the placement of graduates in companies. It can be useful for university managers and for firms to understand whether the presence of Universities on social media by students and firms is positive or not.

Keywords: Social media, social recruitment, job placement, social recruitment in universities

INTRODUCTION

Universities, today, are facing an extremely dynamic and complex environment, which requires the adoption of strategies aimed at continuous change. In order to be "competitive", they need to evaluate and highlight new variables that allow them to respond to the social and cultural evolution. Today, the candidates who are to be placed on the market have got a "digital identity", they spend their free time online on the social networks, they have energy, enthusiasm and know-how, they speak a computer language, they love virtual interaction. In this scenario, the University's main goal, apart from training, becomes that of encouraging its graduates to enter the job market, guaranteeing their placement also with the support of innovative communication tools. In the latest years, the enterprises are progressively changing their recruitment processes abandoning more and more the traditional forms in favor of new processes that guarantee a quality workers profile that measure up to the challenges dictated by globalization and technology.

As a consequence, in order to compete in the "war of talents", Universities have to develop governance behavior and policies influenced by the ICT and its evolutions.

From the publications of Bartram (2000) and Galanaki (2002), on the use of the Internet in the recruitment process, research has grown considerably.

"E-recruitment has been, substantially, influenced by social media" (Schramm, 2007, Kaplan and Haenlein, 2010), which allow companies to look for not only the *"active candidates"* (Furness, 2008; Doherty 2010) but also *"passive candidates"* (Williams and Verhoeven, 2008; Jackson, 2010), through the construction of a relationship based on mutual interest and understanding. (Davison, Maraist and Bing, 2011). The use of social media also allows potential candidates to get to know the brand of the company (Schramm 2007; Dickson and Hollet, 2010) which can show "the human aspect of society" and "an idea about daily activities "(Richards, 2007, Madia, 2010). In this way the job seeker can choose an appropriate employer (Peluchette and Karl, 2010).

Enterprises require from Universities quality candidatures. Therefore, in order to be competitive, Universities, in general, and Career Services, in particular, need to invest in more efficient communication processes, allowing, as a consequence, the internal actors (post-graduates, graduates, students) and the external ones (enterprises) to obtain prompt information. Students, today, place a lot of importance on on-line job search, notification of job posting and communication through electronic means. Therefore the choice of a specific type of communication has obvious social implications: the more the entrepreneurial relationship is based on formality, the more important it will be for the enterprise to speed up the message and thus obtain a quick response. In this global and national picture, the Universities have to face a great challenge, which is not only economical but mainly cultural where social media become the tool for an innovative communication which encourages connection between different cultures, departments and organizations at a distance without time limits, creating in this way new alternatives as opposed to the formal traditions linked to time and space (Peluchette and Karl, 2010). Communication aims at improving the "marketability" of its graduates.

Back in 2001, Davidson showed that the use of the web for career services was convenient. Students had many benefits: they could use it at any-time and in any place, they knew that by using this instrument in private life, they could have direct access to information through the University Career Office front desk.

Although there are many benefits and promises from social media several risks are associated with their use. The ambiguity related to legal and ethical issues (for example individual privacy) of social media at the same time contains the enthusiasm related to the potentialities that social media offer.

This chapter aims at providing an analysis of the phenomenon of social recruitment in four universities of Western Europe through the analysis of the percentage of presence and survival of these social networks and the use of this instrument for the placement of graduates in companies. The purpose of this study is to investigate the different underlying needs and preferences that drive students towards job search and to understand if University Career Services (referred to UCS) use the same instrument. Internet is a territory of millions of social media, such as blogs, social networking, forums, etc. with different subjects, for this reason we have selected only one field of research: Facebook.

This study can be useful for universities managers and for firms to understand whether the presence of Universities on social media by students and firms is positive or not.

2. Facebook's Use in Universities Career Service Offices: An Opportunity or a Risk?

The Job placement service in athenaeums aim at facilitating the entrance of graduates into the working world. By promoting the possibility of getting a job in the world, it lets student and graduates curricula vitae available with the specific aim of gearing them towards jobs. Today, young people aged 22-35 are unemployed and they very often do not look for a job because they know that they will not be able to find it, so the only solution for graduates is competing in a global market. For this reason, many athenaeums have decided to be present and active on social networks. The athenaeums, users of social media, allow their graduates to be more easily identified or introduced for recruitment to managers from enterprises found all over the world. The benefit that can be obtained from this communication and recruitment tool is greatly above its cost and it is superior to traditional methods. In fact, messages sent through social media, besides being more plausible, have a relatively low transmission cost and possess increased applications. The time that enterprises spend in developing relationships that lead to the recruitment of successful candidates can also help in collecting reference information and improving selection. Thanks to the job placement office's simple registration as "fan" on the employer page of an enterprise, all students are signaled within the flow of the enterprise's activity and are visible to the friends on the web. Therefore, this mechanism encourages word of mouth and the diffusion of the contents published. However, in order to let the enterprise may choose its "talents", it is necessary for the candidate to recognize a position within the enterprise where he may grow professionally, where there is a good environment and good

relationships, where he may be appreciated, where his talent may be expressed and where a good balance between work and lifestyle may be maintained. The "employed" enterprise, owner of the web page, has only to create quality contents able to entertain and create buzz marketing on the social web. There is a dual benefit: the "employed" enterprise will directly improve its visibility and image, and there will be an effect on the sale of products. In fact, the methods, the tools and the approaches developed by using social networks for recruitment can be transferred directly to other entrepreneurial functions like marketing, customer services, product development, etc.

The "employer" enterprise, that is, the Athenaeum, improves its visibility by using social networks, and it significantly improves, on the one hand, its perception and, on the other hand, the employment of the most qualified graduates. Thanks to the high visibility of social networks, a high number of qualified candidates can be published who, otherwise, would not have been able to be employed using other sources. Besides, if the high rate of utilities are to be considered as well as the quick answers from enterprises on online social communication channels, the key posts could be filled more quickly, resulting in a reduced number of unemployment of its graduates.

Facebook, today, deeply penetrates users' everyday life and it becomes invisible once it is widely adopted, everywhere, and taken for granted (Luedtke, 2003), so that users do not see its risks. Smith and Kidder (2010) explain how students in universities do not realize that the information they are posting on their profiles and the pictures they are uploading of their experiences can be used by employers as a means of checking up on possible recruitments. Therefore, the main risks are related to privacy and changes in the relationship between public and private spheres, such as inadvertent disclosure of personal information, a damaged reputation due to rumors and gossip, unwanted contact and harassment or stalking, an use of personal data by third-parties, and hacking and identity theft (Boyd & Ellison, 2008).

3. Research Analysis

Search Sample Surveys

In this longitudinal study, we explored the use of social media for job placement in career centres of public universities in four Western European countries through an Internet search. It included the following countries: Italy,

Switzerland, Austria and Germany. Building up the sample surveys of this study has been somewhat laborious.

In order to facilitate the accurate and consistent acquisition of information and to retrieve a comprehensive list of UCS for each country, the first part of the research has been developed directly on the Internet, searching for lists of universities on Wikipedia. Consequently, we consulted country-specific websites with detailed information. If UCS were part of a larger athenaeum with a central office, we explored the central office only. At last, we used Google and each university's website to find additional information such as contact information.

Starting from the panel of the University, a dataset has been created that comprises all Universities, distinguishing them in:

Italy:

- State universities
- Non-state universities but promoted by public authorities (regions, provinces, municipalities)
- University higher education and higher training doctorate institutions that, officially, do not possess degree courses but only doctorates and/or masters
- Non – state universities but recognized by the Ministry of education, by the University

Switzerland:

- Public universities;
- Fachhochschulgesetz (Universities of Applied Sciences);
- Higher Education Institutions of Art and Music;
- Universities of Teacher Education, according to diploma recognition by the EDK / CDIP;
- Federal Institute; according Art. 48 of federal law;
- Other institutions accredited

Austria:

- Federal universities
- Private universities
- Fachhochschulen (University of applied sciences)

Germany:

- Federal State Universities
- Private universities
- Fachhochschule (University of applied sciences)

From this sample only the data relating to public universities were extrapolated, thus, at the end, the sample included 152 public universities overall.

The second part of the research was developed distributing a questionnaire among Career Service Offices. The questionnaire was initially tested on a limited number of offices, in order to understand at which point the questions were correct and the presentation form was accepted. Subsequently, the entire sample survey was posted on the Salento University website and an e-mail with link was sent to career offices. Once a final database was created, sample surveys with questionnaires of this study were built up. In particular, Switzerland sample was composed of eleven career services; Germany of forty career services, while Austria and Italy, respectively, of ten and sixty-five career services (Fig. 1). In total 126 UCS were contacted.

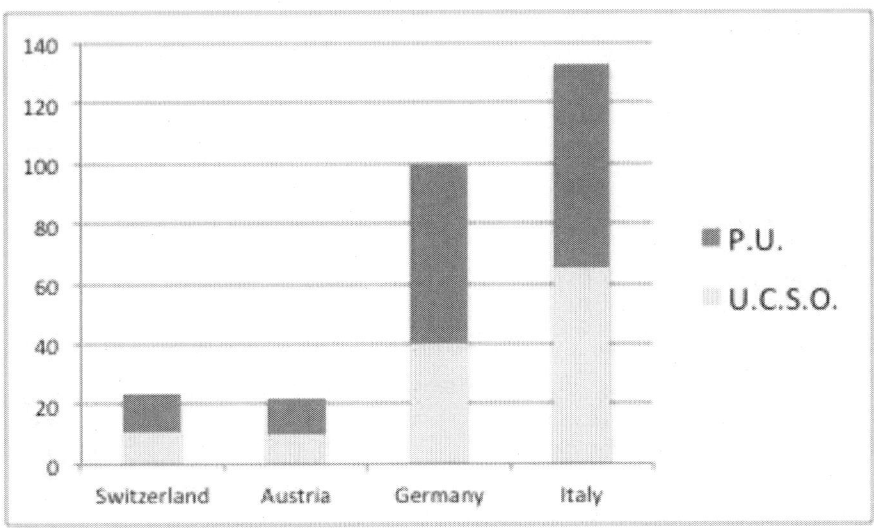

Figure 1. Number of public universities and UCS.

Analysis

The data on opportunities and risks of the social media's use in job placement have been obtained by comparing the analysis of the UCS observations. In order to facilitate the accurate and consistent acquisition of information we have used 5 categories for a total of 16 items to analyze opportunities and risks, measuring them with Likert's technique, in which there are 5 potential answers: 5= strongly agree; 4= Agree; 3=Neutral; 2=disagree; 1= Strongly Disagree, to evaluate the perception.

Each item falls into one of the five categories. The first category is Influence. It concerns the ability of Facebook to influence the choice of job seekers or firms in placement/recruitent process. The second category is Connection. It includes metrics that measure the ability to connect job seekers with the firms or job seekers (students) with UCS to each other. The third category is Access. It examines all the items that minimize barriers between job seekers, firms and UCS. The fourth category is Sharing. It analyzes the capability of Facebook to support hiring process. The last category is Coordination. It includes items that improve job seekers- job seekers, job seekers- firms, firms-UCS coordination. In each categories we have identified if a single item is an opportunity, when the values Ut are positive and higher than 0,5; if it is a risk, when Ut is negative and lower than -0,5; if it is an opportunity/risk, when values range from 0,5 and -0,5– in this case it is necessary that the item is used with competence and caution. For example, "Comment about recruitment process experiences", "Reviews online of firms", "Information on job seeker" and "Information on firm", depend on the accuracy of information. This is true for all the items in which we recognize opportunity/risk.

We listed, then, the answers in a range between x and y, where x is the minimum value of the score attributable to the evaluation (1 = Strongly Disagree) and y the maximum value attributable (5 = strongly agree). Relative advantage, defined Opportunities, (O => [(x+y)/2; y]) refers to the degree to which the adopter perceives the innovation of representing an improvement in either efficiency or effectiveness in comparison to traditional methods. Relative disadvantage, defined Risks, (R => [x; (x+y)/2]) refers to a deterioration.

The sum of the benefits perceived represent the total Utility deriving from the use of Fb in Carrer Service of Universities of single country as means of communication.

Therefore, in order to obtain this value, we have analyzed the values of each item selected and we have created a score for each respondent (UCS). In order to create such utility functions that may represent perceptions for each single item, the average value of the answers given by UCS interviewed was calculated. By so doing, a matrix was created which simply highlighted the resulting evaluations: Total utility (Utility by All Career Services) is positive each time the result of the algebra sum of the Utility by each country becomes positive, while it will be negative when the algebra sum becomes negative. In particular there were 3 positive (Uu was positive); 3 negative (Uu was negative) and in the last case 2 positive and 2 negative (Uu was neutral) (Fig. 2).

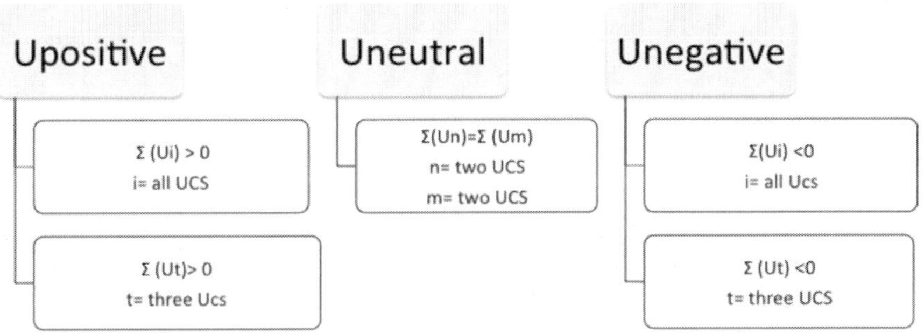

Figure 2. Matrix Utility.

RESULTS

The majority of the analyzed career centres (74,5 % approximately) have been using social media platforms for at least two years and the most used social network is Facebook. This result is similar for all the 4 countries analyzed: Austria 76%, Italy 73%, Germany 75% and Switzerland 74%. In particular 71 % of our sample has a standardized process for the common use of social media websites. That indicates that those 71 % of career centres are aware of the importance of the presence of Fb. The perception about risks and opportunities offered by Facebook is different in the four different countries. Their value is shown in the following figure, considering that the opportunities create a perceived positive utility, while risks a negative utility.

CATEGORIES	ITEMS	**Utotal**		Uaustria	Uitaly	Ugermany	Uswitzerland
Influence	Information on job seeker	**Uneutral**	O/R	2,5	1,6	1,1	1,8
	Information on firm	**Uneutral**	O/R	2,3	2,9	1,9	3,2
Connection	Video or photos of recruitment processes	**Upositive**	O	3,95	4,7	3,8	4,85
	Video or photos of firms	**Upositive**	R	3,9	3,7	3,1	3,9
	Support to confirm the date and the place of recruitment process	**Upositive**	O	3,8	3,1	2,7	2,9
	Improve diffusion of information	**Upositive**	O	3,9	4,7	4,2	4,2
	Comment about recruitment process experiences	**Uneutral**	O/R	3,6	2,9	3,1	2,4
Access	Communication = use of simple language to explain the professional figure to be selected	**Upositive**	O	3,1	3,7	4	2,5
	Communication = use of simple language to explain the hiring process	**Upositive**	O	4,7	4,3	3,3	2,5
	Reviews on line of firms	**Uneutral**	O/R	2,7	2,8	1,6	1,55
Sharing	Sharing of CV	**Upositive**	O	3,9	4,4	3,7	4,8
	Sharing of iter of recruitment processes	**Upositive**	O	3,9	3,2	4	3,6
	Follow some friend's personal placement experience	**Unegative**	R	1,6	1,9	2,4	2
Coordination	Coordination with student	**Upositive**	O	3,9	3,9	4,1	4,3
	Transfer of information fastly and quickly	**Upositive**	O	4	4,4	4,9	2,9
	Ask an appointment	**Upositive**	O	4	4,5	4,2	4,3

Once got this information, we built four "utility functions" that compare the perceptions of the UCS. The graphs (Fig. 3, Fig. 4, Fig. 5 and Fig. 6) highlight the perceptions that the UCS of four countries has about the 16 tested items, divided in categories. In principle, the perceptions regarding the items that fall into the category "Coordination" are similar in Italy, Germany and Switzerland; "Access" and "Connection" are similar in Italy and Switzerland; "Sharing" is similar in Austria and Germany and in Italy and Switzerland, "Information" is similar in Austria, Italy and Switzerland.

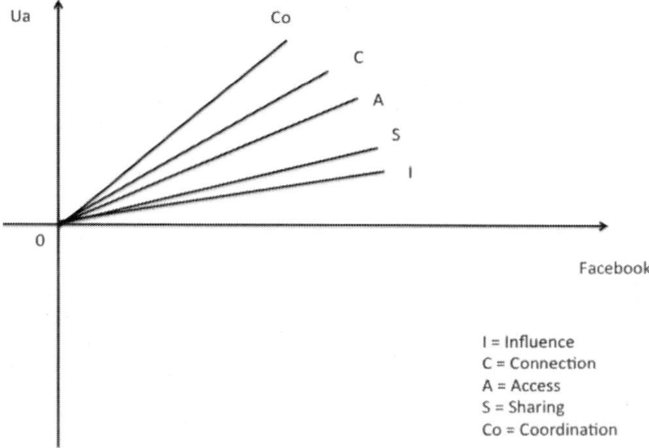

Figure 3. Perception of Utility of Fb by UCS of Austria.

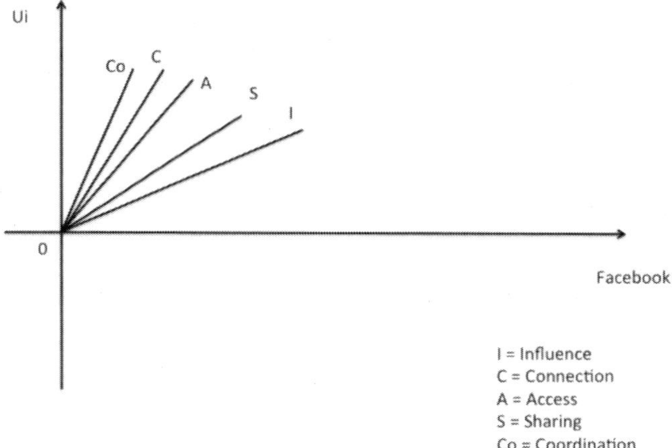

Figure 4. Perception of Utility of Fb by UCS of Italy.

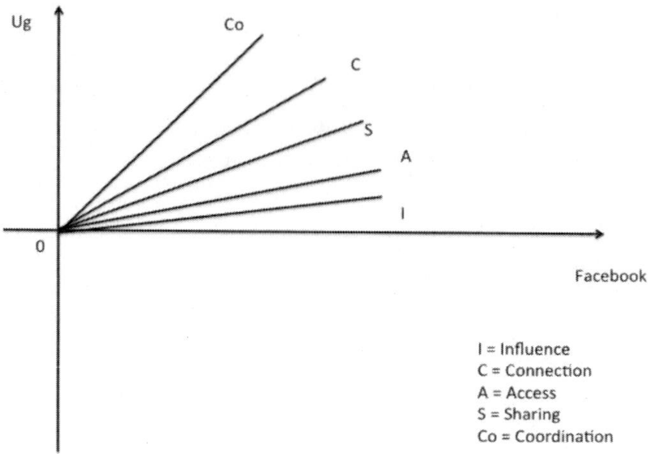

Figure 5. Perception of Utility of Fb by UCS of Germany.

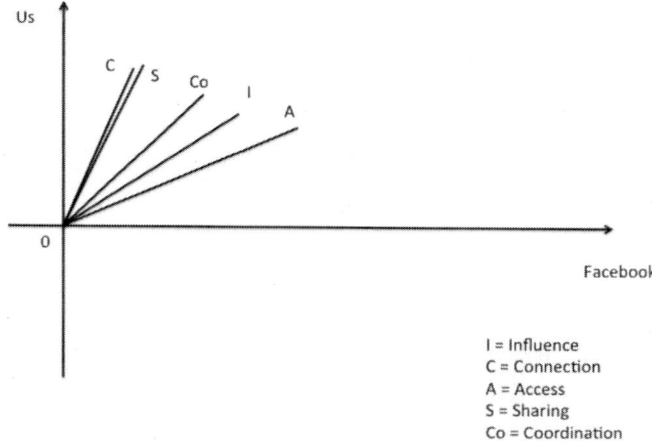

Figure 6. Perception of Utility of Fb by UCS of Switzerland.

Of particular importance is then the graph (Fig. 7) that analyzes the average evaluation of the UCS deriving from the algebraic sum of the two partial Utilities. This analysis indicates that all the UCS of the four countries have a positive perception of the use of Fb. Actually, the values of perceived utility are very similar.

However, we have to highlight that most of the problems Ucs feel about the possible use of Fb are linked to the Information on job seekers and on firms, on the possibility that Comments about recruitment process experiences could be misleading, as well as the reviews online of firms.

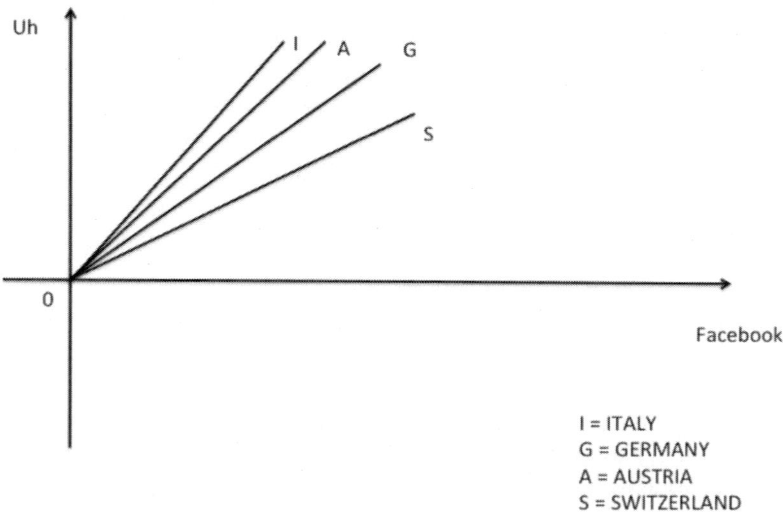

Figure 7. Perception of Utility of Fb of four countries.

CONCLUSION

Today, Universities need to face a dynamic environment that requires constant monitoring and the adoption of changing strategies. In order to be competitive they need to face critically the environmental variables, they need to define strategies in order to react and to efficiently and rapidly enforce them creating a realistic vision for the future. In such circumstances, it is important to develop alternative forms that reflect upon the complexity of the market. Such changes oblige governance to define techniques and strategies that concern the process of recruitment. As a matter of fact, how can it be possible to have a long-lasting competitive advantage if the social and cultural evolution that is changing the young generation's way of thinking is not considered?

Our study shows that in the universities of four countries the perception of the utility of UCS on Facebook is positive. For this reason, the assumptions of traditional job placement of an individual can trap Universities into ways of thinking and action that are not in their best interest.

Career services must adopt a new way of viewing job placement if they wish to remain competitive in the new environment. Facebook allows to create a career portfolio which provides much more flexibility to the students and to the organization.

If we make an hypothesis about the splitting of Universities in:

1. Hyper awake Universities. They are present on Facebook with interactive pages, with videos, posts, and comments to date. They have a link that leads to the "employed pages".
2. Awake Universities. They are present on the social networks but the page is static;
3. Sleep-wake Universities. They have a Facebook page but they use it with irregular attendance (one day in a week, or every three or four days);
4. Dormant Universities. They have not posted any updates in the 30 days preceding the analysis.

It comes out that the Ucs of the four observed countries are "Awake Universities", universities which are present on Fb but which have not fully used Fb potentialities yet, restrained by the fear that what they feel as risks – that is, not complete information – could have on the image of university itself and of students.

This data must not deceive, but make people think. In fact, the items listed as Opportunity/Risk are those requiring a deep reflection on the part of managers and institutions (Figure 8).

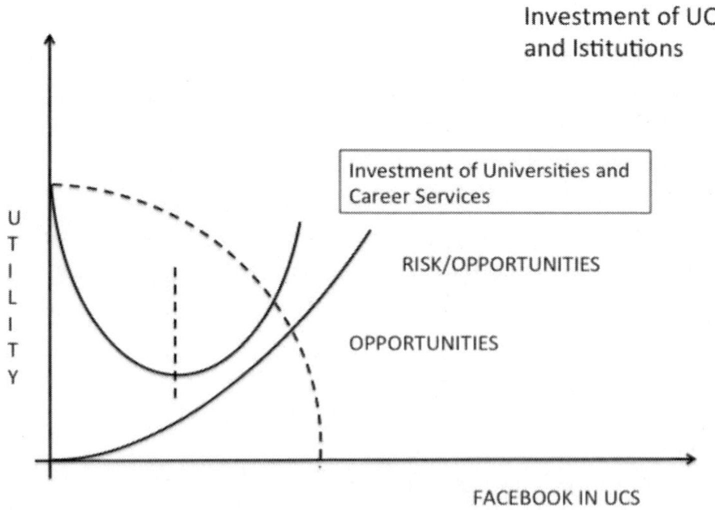

Figure 8. Utility of Facebook in UCS.

Only with investments and laws that clearly define the roles, duties and responsibilities of Facebook users (students, UCS, firms), the possible risks can be transformed into enormous opportunities for all users. By encouraging a correct social media communication, universities can implement their support students and firms in placement activity. In this setting, only organizations that redefine business online (Normann, 1996) will be competitive in long time. In the placement/recruitment process there is often a fine line between caution and fear (as results from our research). The fear of change is so common in this process that universities, students and firms can overcome, developing policies that guide social media use within them. Universities staff members should increment training and education to encourage responsible use of their social media sites. Organizations also must monitor the social media sites to ensure that information posted there does not violate privacy regulations and other laws.

There are important roles for policy makers in supporting social media in placement process. UCS have to guarantee the security of the information presented in social media. Only in these ways we can be sure that information is accurate, timely, relevant and useful for students and firms.

REFERENCES

Amichai-Hamburger Y.e Vinitzky G.,(2010), Social network use and personality, in *Computers in Human Behavior*, 26(6), 1289-1295. Elsevier.

Arboledas, J. R., Ferrero, M.L. and Vidal-Ribas, I. S., (2001), Internet recruiting power: opportunities and effectiveness, University of Navarra, Spain.

Boyd D., Ellison N., (2007), Social network sites: Definition, history, and scholarship, in *Journal of Computer Mediated Communication*, 13(1).

Bartram D., (2000), Internet recruitment and selection: Kissing frogs to find princes, in *International journal of Selection and Assessment*, vol.8, Issue4, December.

Berry B., (2004), Recruiting and retaining 'highly qualified teachers' for hard-to-staff schools, *NASSP Bulletin*, 88 (638).

Boyd D.M. e Ellison N.B., (2007), Social network sites: Definition, history, and scholarship. Journal of Computer-Mediated Communication, 13.

Cappelli P., *On-line recruiting, in Harvard Business Review*, Vol. 79, No. 3, 2001.

Catone, J., (2010), Should Employers Use Social Network Profiles in the Hiring Process?, March 31, retrieved May 7, from http://www.readwriteweb.com/archives/should_employers_use_social_netowrking_when_hiring.phpCatone, 2008

Davidson M.M., (2001), The computerization of career services: Critical issues to consider, in *Journal of Career Development*, 27 (3), 217- 228.

Ellison, N., Steinfield, C., e Lampe, C., (20079, The benefits of Facebook "friends:" Social capital and college students' use of online social network sites. *Journal of Computer-Mediated Communication*, 12.

Furnes V., (2007), *The new frontier, in Personnel Today*, January.

Galanaki E., (2002), The decision to recruit online: a descritive study, in *Career Development International*, vol.17, n.4.

Gravili G., (2008), La cooperazione conveniente: I virtual social networks, Cacucci Editore, Bari.

Gravili G., (2011), *Il social recruitment*, Cacucci Bari.

Kaplan A.M., Haenlein M., (2010) Users of the world, unite! The challenges and opportunities of Social Media - Business horizons, Elsevier.

Hammond, M. S. (2001). Career centers and needs assessments: Getting the information you need to increase your success, in *Journal of Career Development,* 27(3), 187-197.

Lampe C., Ellison N. e Steinfield C., (2007), A familiar Face(book): Profile elements as signals in an online social network, in *Proceedings of the SIGCHI Conference on Human Factors in Computing Systems* (pp. 435-444). New York: ACM Press.

Peluchette J. and Karl K.,(2010) Examining Students' Intended Image on Facebook: "What Were They Thinking?!", in *Journal od Education for Business,* 85: 30–37.

Richards J., (2007) Workers are doing it for themselves: Examining creative employee application of Web 2.0 communication technology, Paper presented at the Work, Employment and Society (WES), 12-14 September 2007, University of Aberdeen, Aberdeen Scotland, http://www.scribd.com/doc/6873217/JRichardsWES2007, 2007

Schramm J., (2007), *Internet connection*, in HRMagazine, vol. 52, n.9.

Valenzuela S., Park N. e Kee K. F.,(2009), Is there social capital in a social network site?: Facebook use and college students' life satisfaction, trust, and participation, in *Journal of Computer-Mediated Communication*, 14(4).

Weigley, S. (2011), Employers recruiting off-campus. The Wall street Journal, In *Wall Street Journal*, 5 August.

In: Social Media
Editor: Annmarie Bennet

ISBN: 978-1-63463-175-4
© 2015 Nova Science Publishers, Inc.

Chapter 4

THE DANGERS OF SOCIAL MEDIA FOR THE PSYCHE

David Brunskill*

Consultant Forensic Psychiatrist
PUAWAI: Midland Regional Forensic
Psychiatric Service, New Zealand

ABSTRACT

This chapter examines how individual users of social media characteristically represent themselves online. It considers whether the process and opportunity for the (apparently) controlled representation of the self online i.e., via the self-selection of favourable visual 'show' material and favourable written 'tell' material, actually has the inherent potential to affect the psyche of the individual and thus represent danger. In doing so, this chapter effectively asks to what extent an improved awareness of the potential for social media to affect the psyche, should actually be the conscious concern of all.

The process of online representation is cumulative, and with respect to social media, effectively creates a socially derived and socially driven, composite online image known as a social avatar. Humans notably select their best aspects for presentation to others, and the self-rendered nature of the social avatar can be seen to reflect this evolutionary tendency, to the extent that social avatars effectively facilitate a psychologically

* Email: david.brunskill@waikatodhb.health.nz.

significant *'gap'* between the online image of an individual (as a hoped for '*representation*' of the self) and their offline identity (as the real '*substance*' of the self).

Social avatars are therefore an important phenomenon to recognise. They function as a simple but effective facilitation mechanism, by which the effects of using social media are delivered to the psyche (including shifts in identity and even psychopathology). Additionally, social avatars have value in the research setting (e.g., they can be dissected to examine levels of narcissism), and conceptual value in the ongoing quest to understand the complicated directional pathways and relationships between social media and the psyche.

This chapter therefore provides a timely overview of the dangers of social media for the psyche and examines the implications for good mental health in the age of cyberspace. It highlights the pervasive influence of social media on identity formation and youth aspiration, and considers the range of negative psychological transformations which can occur. This chapter also raises awareness of what can be an insidious process of psychological erosion, with important human needs such as privacy, authenticity and personal integration, sacrificed along the way - and all with a potential net cost to well-being. In order to achieve an overview (and in a likely reflection of the sprawling nature of social networks themselves), this chapter references a wide range of material including academic research, media commentary, and a selection of the many valuable personal viewpoints which exist 'hidden-away' online.

INTRODUCTION

The human is a profoundly social animal and has a brain to match, so it is not surprising to observe that the many advances in computing technology have been routinely explored for their accompanying social potential. Indeed, the use of the Internet for social purposes has become both an established global phenomenon, and with the development of social media (Table 1 [1]), a highly valued activity within its own right – with registered users of one social network platform alone, conservatively estimated at one billion (or roughly one in seven of the human population). [2]

Paradoxically then, it has been observed that for a medium that has so radically changed the way in which we conduct our lives, the Internet's effects on our psychological health are understudied [3] and research scarce [4]. This has led to the issue of a siren call: That we can no longer ignore the psychological dimensions of going online, and the 'grand experiment with our psyche' that is being conducted [5]. With all experiments there is uncertainty surrounding outcome and what may be gained or lost in the process. This chapter therefore seeks to go beyond the surface picture of the communication benefits enjoyed by many, to explore whether exposure to social media actually represents a danger (i.e., the possibility of injury, pain or loss [6]) to the psyche itself.

Table 1. Social Media – A Definition

Social Media – A Definition
Social Media is an umbrella term (which may end up losing its intrinsic value), it has been defined as: Internet technologies that allow people to connect, communicate and interact in real time to share and exchange information (text, photographs, images, video or audio files). Examples of Social Media include: Social Network Platforms (e.g., Facebook, MySpace) Blogs Twitter Accounts Email Groups and Instant Messaging

Source: adapted from [1].

Social Media Presence and the Importance of Online Image

Image is defined as a symbolic representation and a conception created in the minds of people, especially the general public [6]. It is accorded increasing importance in society and has become established as central and influential to many aspects of modern life, including the online experience. Illustrations of this increasing importance can be found within various different arenas, including the world of business, where the development of a positive corporate image is a clear priority and significant time and resources are expended upon its upkeep and protection. As part of this attention to image, corporate avatars are now being considered and promoted as an important aspect of ensuring a successful business outcome, and an industry offering specialist services in the professional creation and management of online image for company employees has sprung up [7]. Also described, are the emergence of bespoke services who for a fee, can be instructed to act on your behalf as an online reputation concierge, prowling the Web for published dirt on your behalf with the aim of ensuring a clean reputation [5]. It has also been noted that in some occupations, a virtual business profile has replaced a traditional resume to the extent that potential employees must demonstrate a 'strong social media presence' to be considered at all [8].

Further evidence of organisations having an increased awareness of the importance of online image also comes from the healthcare setting, where the development of guidelines for health professionals (in what can be loosely termed as online professionalism) have proliferated [1], [9], [10], [11]. It is also informative to note that such guidance arose from an urgent need being identified for health professionals to be aware of the serious professional consequences that bare-it-all online representations of their views, behaviour and inferred attitudes could have on careers. Clearly then, health professionals and other public servant users of social media must be able to distinguish between "private" and "public" aspects of the material they post to represent themselves, and in this respect then, organisational attention and guidelines can also be seen to herald a more general need for individual users of social media to become more thinking/cognizant of their approach to its use.

Authenticity: The Battleground

Of special note in the corporate application of social media, is the current focus on authenticity as a value, with a steady and notable increase in media interest and commentary urgently promoting authenticity as a subject worthy of marketing attention: 'Engage, don't broadcast. Authenticity and trust are the currency of social media, and they are easier to lose than to win back - Be authentic or go home' [12].

There are dissenting voices too however, and contemporary fiction has richly satirised the attempted exploitation of authenticity as a commercial commodity, and potentially offers up a warning as to the direction the corporate world might be heading:

'Authenticity™ has unparalleled contacts in the world of contemporary cool, we will provide laterally thought-out associative marketing relationships for any company wishing to 'cool up' it's brand. Furthermore, we don't just source cool, we manage it too, providing our clients with an interface they can understand to a world they cannot. We are cool. We own cool. We speak the same language as cool' [13].

Bloggers air doubts too: 'Every social media rulebook hails authenticity as a bastion of success, but is social media killing authenticity?' In rhetorical answer, the social media 'killers' of authenticity are identified to include: 'brevity at the expense of context, out-of-control sharing, a lack of need for accountability, all allied to the truly mobile nature of the technologies'; to the extent that 'being actively conscious of the content you post/disclose risks a point where you filter so much, that the net impact of what's not being said or "softened", creates a facade or persona that no longer accurately reflects who you really are' [14].

Whilst it is agreed that the relationship between social media and authenticity is indeed of note, from a psychiatrist's perspective, it is currently misplaced; and a pliant term has been twisted to suit – a one night stand between the freely harnessed beast of social media and the shiny cart of business if you will. This chapter therefore offers up a re-examination of the original concept of authenticity including as it relates to social media, but with due reference to its original psychological perspective. In this way it aims to allow the true value of authenticity – i.e., as it relates to the human condition - to re-surface, be revived, and hopefully be reclaimed, so that the question and emphasis shifts; *From*: Am I being authentic enough in my social media communications and marketing to ensure brand consistency and business success? *To*: Does social media affect my authenticity as an individual, and thus my wellbeing?

For when the relationship between authenticity and social media is examined from a mental health perspective, there is a sense that a valuable concept is being firmly hijacked and cheapened along the way, with all the inherent potential the concept actually had to teach us about good mental health in cyberspace, alarmingly close to being jettisoned for good. Essentially seen as an extension of higher order psychological needs such as self-actualization [15], and with due reference to the psychological importance placed on the need for congruence between one's self behaviour and one's self image in the development of the 'ideal self' [16], authenticity has been defined as: 'the unobstructed operation of one's true or core self in one's daily enterprise' [17]. 'Psychological' authenticity is therefore considered to comprise of four components (Table 2).

So where does this re-clarification leave the *actual* relationship between authenticity and social media?

It seems clear from the analysis presented in Table 2 [17], that social media has the potential to affect all four components of authenticity separately, or as a related whole. Simply put, social media does not appear designed to promote/enhance psychological authenticity, as negative material being chosen to represent the self is highly unlikely to see the monitor.

In terms of why this matters, research has shown that those individuals with higher total scores on Authenticity Inventories (AI), actually report higher levels of self esteem and life satisfaction, with researchers concluding that 'empirical support exists for the contention that authenticity is indeed related to a healthy psychological function and positive subjective wellbeing' [17]. A related question must therefore be, what sort of a relationship does social media encourage a user to develop with their real self?

Table 2. The Four Components of Authenticity

Authenticity Component	Component Description
Awareness	Awareness involves knowledge and acceptance of one's multifaceted and potentially contradictory self-aspects (polarities), as opposed to rigid acceptance of only those aspects deemed internally consistent with one's overall self-concept *(in other words: nobody is perfect)*
Unbiased Processing	Unbiased processing is an objective appraisal of one's positive and negative self-aspects, attributes, qualities and potentials (no denial/distortion/exaggeration)
Behaviour or Action	Reflects acting in accordance with one's values, preferences and needs (congruent), as opposed to acting merely to please others or to attain rewards or avoid punishments, even if it means acting falsely (incongruent)
Relational	Relational authenticity involves an active process of self-disclosure and the development of mutual intimacy and trust so that intimates will see one's true self-aspects, *both good and bad*

Source: adapted from [17].

Perhaps a story from real life can help think this through. The following narrative was posted in a public online forum, and makes for an interesting, if ultimately cautionary read, as it outlines a personal experience of living with a depression, and bravely reports on a personal journey from 'living in-authentically to living authentically', and the difference it made: *"I was able to project a successful image to the outside world but I knew that my life was an illusion. I was very unhappy because I was trying to be who I thought would be acceptable to others, rather than live my life in a way which pleased myself, and not according to a false image of success that had formed in my psyche over years of conditioning"* [18].

This narrative then, has clear parallels to the actual relationship authenticity has with social media, as it relates a real life example of a psychologically significant gap between external appearance (akin to online image) and the emotional reality on the inside of the person and their home (akin to the offline substance of the self). It is also an effective example of the (growing) human tendency to prize image over substance and to use projection to overcome personal reality. The narrative's conclusion (that authentic living could be a key to improved happiness for many living with depression, as authentic people are living according to their own values [18]), therefore functions as a stark warning for those individuals whose social media use also translates to a similarly large gap between their offline reality and their online image.

THE 'SUNDAY BEST' PHENOMENON: ONLINE ASPECTS OF PERSONAL IDENTITY AND IMAGE

Identity refers to the individual characteristics which define a person, or by which a person can be recognized [6]. Unlike image, identity is therefore more of an essence than a representation. On an individual level, defining one's personal identity has become increasingly multi-faceted and complicated, with many contributing strands. Factors relevant to this development include an observable increase in the number of social roles available for the individual and perhaps, shifting societal expectations also (e.g., with respect to age, gender and multicultural community influences). In addition to these societal based developments, personal identity will increasingly and inevitably come to include online aspects of image also (particularly in the case of youth, as this chapter will explore later).

The striving for a positive self-presentation is a notable human tendency. It can be seen to have its roots in terms of the evolutionary advantages that a positive self-presentation can have, and is also considered to be linked to the related human need to 'develop and maintain a reasonably positive self-esteem' [4].

It is also important to acknowledge that, given a choice, the tendency for humans to characteristically choose favourable material to represent the self is nothing new (late Victorian Britain for example, was characterised by a need to select the best aspects of one's personal situation for presentation to others e.g., wearing "Sunday Best" clothes for church, receiving visitors in a "Best Room" and reserving the "Best China" for them to take tea in). However, it does appear that the advent and development of cyberspace has been something of a game-changer, with the Internet being described as being 'capable of facilitating dramatic shifts in identity and behaviour, and is an immersive medium with the power to transform well-worn activities into novel ones' [5]. Thus, social network platforms allow its users a previously unavailable level of personal image control and a blank screen for the projection of aspects of their personal identity in novel and powerful ways and are an ideal setting for the encompassing business of image management.

The use of personalised websites/social networks is not the sole gateway to the construction of identity however, as personal image management has always been attended to (and still is) in offline social interactions as well. Indeed, chinks in image and identity are perhaps more readily glimpsed offline, as in this poetic description from a pop-star of their 'pet peeve': "*When you see somebody's façade. When you are in a room of people who are trying to be someone other than themselves in order to be accepted...the misty mirror in front of people's identities*" [19].

What does seem clear is that the construction of identity is a complex psychic endeavour. It has been highlighted that whilst face-to-face identity construction and identity announcement must be consistent with physical characteristics; in online settings such as social networks, individuals can manage image and control their identity towards a hoped for ideal of the possible self [4].

In other words, whereas the offline/real life actualization of the hoped-for possible self can be scuppered by difficult to change physical characteristics and personal dispositions, social networks offer the user the chance to get round these stubborn aspects via the judicious use of personal control. It is also interesting to note that some commentators even question the received wisdom that users actually possess the degree of control they imagine in presentation of the self online: 'This is the horror of social media – it gives us the impression we are in control of our virtual identities, putting out messages that chime with our "real" selves or some idealized version of them, whereas in fact there is always slippage and leakage, the subconscious asserting its obscure power' [20].

THE INTERFACE BETWEEN THE ONLINE MEDIUM AND THE INDIVIDUAL USER

In order to explore specific psychological aspects of going online (such as the effects of social media upon the psyche), it is also necessary to consider the forces which might govern and influence our online behaviours; both those specific to the *medium*, and also those related to the *individual* user.

Fundamental to understanding this process, is the long standing recognition that the online setting is a medium which exerts a multi-factorial disinhibiting influence on all (Table 3), and that the 'online disinhibition effect' [21], should therefore be considered as the backdrop for social media use. The case has also been made that the medium itself has the power to fundamentally change the personality of the user (the e-personality) [5].

Table 3. The Disinhibition Effect

Has benign and toxic forms and is considered to related to specific aspects on the online medium itself including: Anonymity Invisibility The asynchronous nature of communication The induced experience of dissociation The perceived equality of all users - encouraging the minimizing of legitimate authority

Source: adapted from [21].

The origins of social networks themselves are also worthy of consideration; for example the prototypical website facemash (also from the creator of facebook) was created by hacking into House online facebooks and compiling ID photos onto the facemash website, allowing viewers to vote for the "hotter" of two randomly chosen photos, or rate the looks of students in a particular House against fellow residents [22]. Clearly then, based on this prelude, social networks have been intrinsically concerned with image as a property from their very conception, and it is therefore unsurprising that in time, with the offer of full self-presentational control to the user, social media/social networks have developed into a context where 'it is both acceptable and the norm to use such features to boast' [4].

On an individual level, it has been proposed that five interlocking factors can help observers to understand how individuals manage who they are in cyberspace [23] (Table 4). Thus it appears likely that the personality of the individual is another important consideration (i.e., an individual's use of cyberspace - as in many other areas of life - is likely to reflect the characteristics of their personality). Building on this notion, it has been further hypothesised that individuals with specific personality traits/clusters may potentially express themselves in a characteristic fashion online [24] (Table 5), although the need for significant further research into this aspect has been noted.

Table 4. Factors influencing identity management in cyberspace

Level of dissociation and integration	The multiple aspects of one's identity may be dissociated, enhanced, or integrated online
Positive and negative valence	Negative aspects of one's identity can be acted out or worked through. Positive aspects can be expressed and developed
Level of fantasy or reality	One's online identity can be real-to-life, imaginary or hidden
Level of conscious awareness and control	People differ in how much their unconscious needs and emotions surface in their online attitudes
The (Social) Media chosen	Different communication channels express different aspects of identity

Source: adapted from [23].

Table 5. How Personality Type could be related to Characteristic Behaviour Online

Personality Type	Characteristic Behaviour Online
Schizoid	Attracted by the reduced intimacy resulting from online anonymity
Antisocial	Exploits anonymity for own advantage/gain
Narcissistic	Accesses multiple relationships as a means to increase the potential for admiration
Histrionic	Uses online groups as a stage for expression
Passive-Aggressive	Uses online groups to forcefully disagree/oppose
Dissociative	Online identity split off from face-to-face identity

Source: adapted from [24].

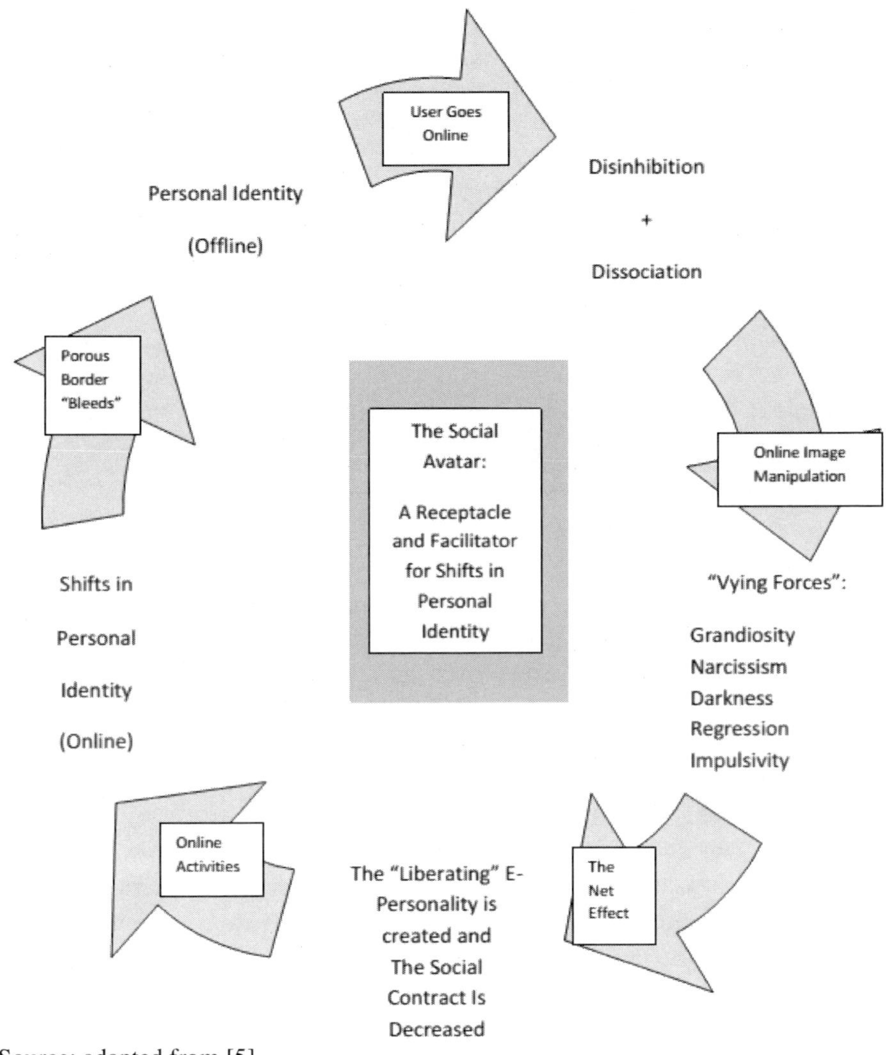

Source: adapted from [5].

Figure 1. The Social Avatar Facilitates Shifts In Personal Identity.

Given the complex nature of these interfaces though, outlining a cohesive and unifying explanatory mechanism for psychological transformation, is both a challenge of terminology and of process. However, in an attempted summary, the following observations have been made [5]:

Going online results in a state of disinhibited and dissociated personhood, and this state is the foundation on which a distinct 'e-personality' develops (the e-personality is a virtual whole which is greater than its parts; and despite not being real, full of life and vitality, existing as it does alongside traditional offline personality, but with the liberating advantages of being unfettered by either old rules or the wider social contract). Five psychological forces (Grandiosity, Narcissism, Darkness, Regression and Impulsivity) then vie to assert themselves as the material from which the e-personality is built, and they - in a twenty first century confirmation of the Freudian id - cause a psychological transformation (and fracture) in personal identity, known as the Net Effect [5].

This chapter therefore builds on these ideas by proposing that in order for such changes in personal identity and psychological transformations to occur, there needs to be an appropriate receptacle/facilitator/delivery system, and that this is the social avatar (Figure 1).

Avatars and Social Avatars: Characteristics and Psychological Importance

Having considered such issues as image, identity and the interface of the medium with the individual, this chapter will now examine the way in which the human user represents the self in cyberspace; a process which has been described as 'fascinating, complex and with respect to our human nature, ultimately revealing' [25].

In seeking to explore the phenomenon of self-representation online, the term "avatar" is a key concept to recognise and understand. The term avatar is defined as 'an earthly incarnation of a Hindu deity' [6]. Over recent years though, this term has been borrowed to describe the way in which human users represent themselves on a computer. Whilst the first avatars created were basic, those currently utilised by computer gamers in cyberspace arenas such as the massively multiplayer online role-playing games (MMORG's), can be extensively customised and are bespoke and interactive. The virtual online world of cyberspace has become well developed, and with the advent of social media providing a significant opportunity for self-representation, the term avatar has been firmly hijacked and expanded in definition to include: One's personal manifestation in a virtual world - the image you create for yourself, as well as the psychological character or persona you present to others [26].

In 2013, a further extension to the hijacked term avatar was proposed, with the prefix of "social" used to denote the representation of the self online, with reference to the widespread use of social media/social network platforms which incorporate the opportunity for online image control via the self-selection of representational material. It was described that 'inherent to the experience of using social media, is the self-selection of favourable material to represent the individual (likely in varying degrees of conscious awareness). This process is cumulative, and effectively creates a socially derived and socially driven, composite online image, also known as the social avatar' [27].

The human tendency towards favourable representation has already been noted and when this tendency is allied to the opportunities made available online, it has been described that 'giving free reign to our imagination allows it to imbue our ambassador in cyberspace with special attributes of intelligence, status, and charisma which we do not normally possess nearly to the same degree' [5]. That the Internet broadly allows us to re-invent portions of ourselves that we are not happy with therefore seems abundantly clear, and social avatars can be expected to reflect this by being predominantly concerned with self-promotion.

Integral to complex gaming and social media network platforms, is the requirement for an interactive virtual persona to allow user interaction with others - either as overtly created avatars (such as those constructed in Second Life and The Palace), or as subtler and more covertly created social avatars (such as those constructed on Facebook and Myspace). For both avatars and social avatars, it is their self-selected and self-rendered nature that gives the process psychological significance, and this has been demonstrated by research in interesting ways. For example, a 2009 study found that when participants chose a provocative avatar to present their virtual identity to others (participants could vary their bodily characteristics to include a high bust/hip ratio, skimpy clothing and navel piercings), this was independently associated with online sexual advances towards the participant who had created and was represented by the provocative avatar in question [28].

This type of behavioural finding (of a self-fulfilling prophesy) indicates that avatars and social avatars can shape the behaviours of both the user/presenter and the receiver/perceiver, a concept which has been termed the Proteus Effect [29]. Social avatars, however, probably go a step further in that social media network platforms (which clearly allow users an even greater degree of personalisation - with written descriptions, narratives, photographs and other social information based on visible associations), effectively form the basis of a more extensive, bespoke and personally meaningful representation of the self. It has also been noted that this can get out of hand, with over attention and obsession with this area by users of social media drawing stinging criticism from populist media. Indeed, 'Iconization', or 'caring too much about your cover/avatar/icon and updating it with nanoscopic changes no one else cares about', is considered to be one of the '25 Worst Things about Social Media' [30]. It therefore seems highly likely - and a serious oversight in the context of the potential for social media to represent a danger to the psyche - that users give more thought to their choice of avatar/social avatar material, than they do as to how their psyche could be being affected by this process. This chapter will now focus on why this is considered psychologically risky, and why this imbalance must be rectified.

Identifying the Potential Dangers of Social Media for the Psyche (Direct and Indirect)

Antisocial Behaviour Online and Cyberbullying

That the Internet can serve as a tool that can enhance wellbeing is accepted; likewise obvious advances in communication are clearly enjoyed by many. However, problems related to social media continue to emerge and appear to both match the pace of technological advance, and reflect the dark side of human behaviour also. Posted material designed to be damaging and offensive to others can be varied, inventive and designed for maximum impact (as an example of subversive - likely pathological - online behaviour, the use of anonymity to troll memorial internet groups in order to deface online obituaries seems hard to beat).

Cyber-bullying, unwanted/inappropriate contact, the posting of inappropriate/distressing information and problems related to the concept of addiction have all been identified as online behaviours which can have a negative impact in the general population [31]. Not surprisingly then, given that the majority of the above examples effect the psyche of users indirectly i.e., via the antisocial behaviour of other users, the guidance for positive online social networking which does exist, tends to have a narrow psychological focus, such as general safety tips for users [32].

Whilst a full discussion of the emerging phenomenon of cyberbullying (i.e., the use of electronic devices to over-power others) is beyond the scope of the chapter, it represents a startlingly clear example of how social media can affect the psyche of those involved in profound ways. Worryingly, research considers cyberbullying to be on the rise and to 'afford several advantages over traditional bullying' [33]. It is also considered that the approach to cyberbullying necessitates additional interventions to those used for traditional bullying, and specific tactics to keep up with the unanticipated opportunities for social interactions, positive and negative, available through diverse media [33].

Problematic Internet Use (PIU)

Current research efforts related to the psychological dimensions of going online are mostly focussed on its direct effects in the form of its addictive potential. For example, the concept of Internet Gaming Disorder – a term considered analogous to the popularly dubbed 'Internet Addiction', has a proposed criteria set and designation as a condition for further study in DSM-V [34]. However, whilst this is a necessary avenue for further research with a focus on treatment, this situation is narrow in two ways: Firstly, it raises the potential for an internet-related condition to exist, without any apparent reference to the vast use of social media and the presumed potential this also has to be 'addictive' akin to gaming. Secondly, this focus distracts and diverts attention away from the many notes of concern which go beyond the addiction model of interference with function. This apparent position of over-sight has therefore attracted critique, both with respect to the concept of Internet Addiction itself, 'a blunt-edged label, glossing over the actual needs being fulfilled, or the insecurities which already exist within us' [5], but also its distracting effects too: 'taking valuable attention away from the subtle ways in which the Internet can affect the psychology of all its users - including non-addicts' [5].

The working term and addiction related concept of Problematic Internet Usage (PIU) is also up and running [3], and is beginning to move towards a definition and perhaps more importantly, highlighting the potential for nuances along the pathway to the clinical condition. Researchers have therefore described PIU as 'best conceptualized not as a unitary mental health condition at all, but as a complex end-point behaviour of a plethora of underlying psychological, developmental, ecological and intra-familial factors' [35]. Furthermore, in considering youth, it has also been highlighted that the (so called) generation wired 'are already beginning to view the virtual world as more "real" (i.e., more meaningful) to them than what the preceding generation would term "reality" – to the extent that PIU can be rightly considered to be the ultimate post-modern affliction of the 21st century' [35].

Negative Psychological Transformations

Although an awareness of the more overt/obvious effects of social media upon the psyche is obviously important (e.g., via the dysfunctional postings/antisocial online behaviour of others, and the potential for 'addiction'), the subtler psychological effects of the online experience should also be considered. The following is a selected description of the negative psychological transformations which are thought to occur.

Identity Shifts and Compartmentalization

The Internet's facilitation of shifts in personal identity and behaviour does appear to have been largely insidious, leading to the observation that 'for all the change wrought by the virtual world, the subtle reconfiguring of our psychological landscape that has taken place along the way appears lost on us, and the very significant and often negative psychological transformations that have ensued have gone largely unexplored' [5].

Examples of these negative psychological transformations can actually be readily identified, and indeed can be found in obvious places, such as with respect to individuals who already struggle to integrate aspects of their personal identity. Thus, specific concerns have been identified which range from the concrete (the Internet has been incorporated into delusions by some individuals [31]), to the abstract, (the creation of a social avatar creates compartmentalization and reinforcement of pre-existing pathological divisions within the self [27]). Compartmentalization has been traditionally defined in pathological terms as keeping separate parts of one's personality that should be kept together [36]. Whilst it may alternatively be conceived of as an everyday defence mechanism - serving to increase efficiency in a world with complex and competing demands on our time and emotions - such compartments will clearly need to be periodically processed in order for an authentic psychological self to thrive and the personal integration necessary for good mental health to occur.

Congruence and Incongruence

Consciously or unconsciously, people conceal or misrepresent aspects of their self as often as they honestly reveal them.

This process (of revealing something while hiding something else) is known as compromise formation [21] and has direct relevance to the use of social media, where the self-selection of representational material is inherent to the experience. By selecting/omitting the written, visual, and audio material to represent the self online, social media provides an opportunity to project an ideal, or hoped for version of the self (perhaps without the inhibiting influences which could ordinarily be expected to result from physical processes such as reality-checking and face to face feedback from others).

By selecting the best bits to represent the self in the creation of a social avatar, online image is therefore highly unlikely to match offline identity, and a psychologically significant "gap" is created (Figure 2), with an obvious potential to contribute to internal conflict, emotional distress, and a psychological erosion of the congruence necessary for psychological authenticity and well-being in the longer term.

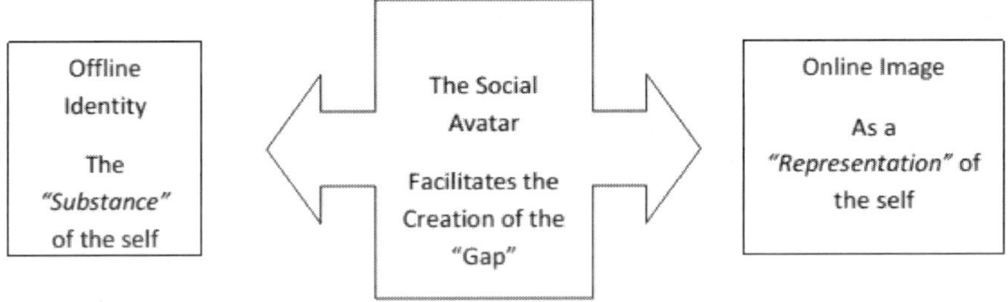

Figure 2. The Social Avatar Facilitates the Creation of a Psychologically Significant 'Gap'.

Acting out

Cyberspace has been described as a psychological extension of the individual's intra-psychic world and a psychological space that can stimulate the processes of projection, acting out and transference [24]. Case reports from different settings illustrate this observation further: In court, the use of a social avatar resulted in a pathologically increased need to save face [37]. In psychoanalysis, presenting one version of the self in person and another via social media resulted in an accompanying (and unhelpful) expectation that the two would remain un-integrated in treatment [38]. It is also intriguing to consider whether the application of psychodynamic thinking may also have the potential to spotlight the psychological make- up of those who use the Internet in deeply harmful ways towards others.

Could cyberbullying for example, be considered in terms of the size of the gap which exists in the perpetrator between offline identity and online image, and the projection of this conflict/inadequacy on to the victim?

Unhelpful Emotional States

As part of the social media experience, the social avatar (and the psychologically significant gap it represents) may be implicated in contributing to unhelpful emotional states within the individual user. For example, by inviting ongoing comparisons with the projected/inflated /exaggerated lifestyles of others, there is clearly a potential for an unhelpful sense of dissatisfaction to result in the social media user. Indeed, envy, jealousy and depression are all anecdotally reported with respect to the online and artificial process of comparison, including in the context of the coarse measures of implied popularity which are inherent to social media platforms (e.g., the numbers of advertised "friends", or "likes" in response to a user's postings).

This has led some to observe that depression in the context of social media is a type of 'smiling depression' [8], with roots in the gap between the externalities of online image and the emotional reality of the internal state. Evidence of social media affecting the psyche can also be demonstrated by inference, such as when the gap between online image and offline substance is exposed for what it is, with negative results such as 'difficult-to-take, psychologically violent, and very rude awakenings' [5] and 'desperate attempts to save face [37] having been reported.

Whilst at first glance then, social media and the creation of a social avatar is an intoxicating opportunity offering significant freedoms (including the illusion of personal control), on further analysis, it appears to actually come with its own *psychological pressures*.

For example, the narcissistic pressure to conform (everyone else's virtual identity is above average also [5]), and that individuals run a risk of exhaustion secondary to putting their lives on constant display for fear of missing out (FOMO) [39], itself related to the clear expectation of participation that accompanies the 'connected' status.

NARCISSISM: RELATIONSHIP TO SOCIAL MEDIA AND SOCIAL AVATARS

Narcissism refers to an inflated sense of the self (clever, attractive, capable, powerful etc.), and ultimately, one's own importance. Many downstream effects stem from this, such as in relationships (superficial rather than deep), and where a sense of entitlement can be expressed. A pattern of people essentially being used for the fulfilment of one's own narcissistic needs (to be admired, acknowledged as special and unique) is then formed. Narcissists are also interested in opportunities to look good including through association and can therefore be found where there is credit to be taken (including in the reflected glory of others) and popularity to be accrued.

The concept of narcissism has been taken from the individual and successfully applied to society, and the resultant findings have been far in range and reach. A broad range of cultural symptoms are therefore considered to represent a 'narcissism epidemic' and include: 'Increased materialism and entitlement, increased rates of plastic surgery and credit card debt, the use of "my" in web addresses and the rising square footage of residences' [40]. This situation is further considered to have come about courtesy of 'the rise of the self-esteem movement, the advent of the internet, and the emergence of the celebrity lifestyle as something to aspire to and endorse [40].

Indeed, it was anticipated by researchers that the opportunity for an interactive personalised webpage would be of interest to a narcissistic individual (where the level of personal control over self-presentation is seemingly unparalleled) and this has been borne out, with research concluding that narcissists 'act, portray themselves, and are perceived on social networking sites in a manner similar to how they behave in real, offline life', [41] and that narcissism also 'predicts higher levels of social activity in the online community, and more self-promoting content' [41] (such as attractive photos and glowing written descriptions of the self).

Such research is also thought to support the notion that social networks are satisfying for narcissists because they allow for controlled self-presentation, satiate the craving for attention and are concerned with the accruement and promotion of shallow relationships. Intriguingly, significant differences between the genders have also been found: (males with high narcissism scores display more descriptive self-promotion via 'About Me' quotes; females with high narcissism scores display more superficial self-promotion via 'Main Photos' selection) [4].

This chapter also notes with interest that such studies into narcissism and social media use can be seen to have systematically broken down individual profiles (from their composite form into the constituent parts of the visual and written material posted to represent the self), and that this is effectively a *dissection of the social avatar* which then allows for the material to be rated for its self-promoting nature.

As well as sustaining the interest of researchers, media interest in narcissism also shows no signs of slowing, and why would it when the culture it surveys delivers a bona-fide new word: "*Selfie*" - defined as a photograph that one has taken of oneself with a smartphone or webcam and uploaded to a social media website - was chosen as the Oxford Dictionary's Word of the Year in 2013 [42]. Indeed, the selfie has come to be considered by some as 'the ultimate emblem of the age of narcissism' [43] (with examples cited to support this, such as a selfie taken at a funeral with the accompanying text: 'Love my hair today, hate why I'm dressed up') [43].

Such blatant and taboo-busting self-promotion probably used to be generationally described as 'showing off', a behaviour which is currently considered to be: 'never easier and, ironically, more celebrated - we are in unchartered waters of egotistic adulation' [44]. To be fair to media commentators though, there is often real concern and thought to be found underneath journalistic headlines e.g., 'like so much else in the digital world, it seems all about me, but reveals a desperate urge to find an us' [43], and that 'online manifestations of narcissism may be little more than a self-presentational strategy to compensate for a low and fragile self-esteem' [44].

Modern Fame and Celebrity Worship

Social media also seems to have become steadily intertwined and enmeshed with celebrity culture; at the same time that what constitutes modern celebrity, has been stretched beyond meaning to an 'empty celebrity cult, which worships people just because they are famous, regardless of whether fame is inherited, achieved, or ascribed' [45]. The point has also been made that reinforcement occurs in a cyclical fashion as 'social media allows everyone to tweet, broadcast and blog as if they were celebrities, creating an alternate reality and turning friends, acquaintances, strangers (? even family – author's addition) into fans and followers' [45]; all topped off by the fact that celebrities use the same platforms to do the same thing.

There is also the small matter of children, with evidence emerging that becoming famous has become *the* major aspiration of children from 10-12 years of age, following the values for fame becoming prevalent in popular media (TV), with 'a lifestyle of enormous success, wealth and renown being depicted as normative for adolescent characters, which can then be duly enacted out on video-sharing social media platforms such as YouTube' [46]. A survey into social media by the same research team (CDMC@LA) has also been reported in the media, as having found that 'young people who use social media place a higher value on fame than kids who don't use it or use it infrequently' [47].

Digital Natives and Digital Naivety

If there was ever a doubt that the digital landscape in some countries and cultures is all encompassing, this must surely be quelled by the (NY Times) reported practice of setting up a digital presence for those just born [48]. When considering such developments from a mental health perspective, whilst they may seem innocent, they also appear to be poorly thought through - in that in the above example, any ramifications will not be identifiable for roughly a decade, and thus have a distinctly experimental quality to them by definition. In considering examples such as this, this chapter highlights that essentially, the *duality* within our use of the internet and social media (*good for us/bad for us*), does not appear to be a message that is being heard. Perhaps the best that can be currently hoped for is that such experiments have the (no doubt) intended effect of providing delight rather than damage; but when a duality exists, the outcome is always uncertain.

Identity Formation in the Wired Generation

It seems inevitable then, that the opportunity for self-presentation via social media will have a certain synergy with identity formation. In this regard, quotes from the past can be instructive and appear eerily pre-emptive: 'The playing adult steps sideward into another reality; the playing child advances forward to new stages of mastery' [49].

But does the internet enhance or hinder this mastery? This chapter has already highlighted research that demonstrates the capacity of the internet and social media to be influential (as per the example of fame climbing the ladder to the top of youth aspirations [46]). In many ways, this is logical, as if there are indeed effects upon the psyche, the adolescent demographic may be particularly vulnerable; being both among the heaviest, and most avant-garde users of social media, and during a crucial period of development too.

The essential identity question being faced by young people has been put in deceptively simple terms as: *What kind of self can (or should) I become?* [50]. Seminal work into the crisis of identity (Erikson) has been further classified into 'identity statuses' including: Identity Diffusion (unquestioning, not committed), Foreclosure (prematurely committed without exploration), Moratorium (experiencing an intense exploration, or identity crisis) and Identity Achievement (careful consideration has led to a firm commitment in things such as occupation and ideology) [51].

Additionally, the adolescent's progress toward the desired outcome (of identity achievement) is thought to be influenced by four factors or domains (Table 6).

Table 6. The Factors Influencing Identity Formation

Factor	Influence
Cognitive	Intellectual maturity assists identity formation (complex cognitive task)
Parenting	The quality of the adolescent-parent relationship is important
Scholastic	Can both move identity formation forwards towards maturity and backwards (regression)
Social-Cultural	Some cultures create identity foreclosure (non-questioning), some cultures encourage 'questioning' along the way

Source: adapted from [50].

Given that using online activities to explore and change identities was described as a 'fairly common pursuit' in the early 2000's [50], it can be safely assumed to be at least common by now, and most likely heading towards the norm in certain cultures and countries. It therefore follows that arguably the biggest change in the four factors considered in Table 6 have been in the 'social-cultural' domain, and specifically with reference to the advent of the now ubiquitous online world and the speedy rise of its social applications. As prominent researchers have put it, 'Media, ever present in the lives of today's youth, are an important source of information for the developing contexts of what the social world outside their immediate environment is all about' [52]. In other words, media (and social media) appears to have developed into *the* social-cultural factor influencing identity formation, and this has researchers worried in terms of the potential for significant downstream effects [52].

Social media (and the internet) therefore has the capacity to be influential during every stage of dynamic identity formation, and appears likely to directly contribute to the fluxes which are part of the modern adolescent experience for many (and thus potentially an agent of change: for better or for worse). It should also be a note of concern, that at the same time this socio-cultural aspect is providing substrate and context for an essential developmental phase, it is also simultaneously providing related opportunities for cyber-bullying.

Privacy: Loss and Function

At times then, the rise of the internet and social media, seems to be a case of taking with one hand and giving with the other - as in this observation: 'Google knows what you are looking for. Facebook knows what you like. Sharing is the norm, and secrecy is out. But what is the psychological and cultural fallout from the end of privacy?' [20] Interestingly, the answer may be best given in terms of what you lose along the way: 'Privacy, precisely because it ensures that we are never fully known to others, provides a shelter for imaginative freedom, curiosity and self-reflection' [53].

One way of thinking about where privacy might fit into the psyche (and by extension to consider what exactly is being threatened by mass social media uptake and self-promotion), is via the Johari Window [54], described as 'a neat way of categorising what are the conscious and subconscious areas in one's life' [55] (Table 7).

Table 7. The Johari Window

	What you see in me	What you do not see in me
What I see in me	The Public Self	The Private Self
What I do not see in me	The Blind Self	The Unknown Self (Mystery)

Source: adapted from [54] and [55].

The loss of privacy as something to lament seems to be further confirmed on an individual basis too: 'One's constant expression via social media leads to a dissipation of creative energy and *loss* of the valuable incubation time necessary for creative ideas' [56].

CONCLUSION

Inherent to the experience of using social media is the self-selection of favourable material to represent the self via a show and tell process. This creates a social avatar which is positively skewed in keeping with the human evolutionary tendency towards the selection of best aspects for presentation to others (the anatomy of the psyche sees individuals naturally accept positive aspects of the self as valid aspects of who they are, in preference to unpleasant aspects which may be rejected or psychologically defended against). Thus, the nature of a social avatar reflects this tendency and facilitates the creation of a psychologically significant gap between online image (as a *representation* of the self) and offline identity (as the *substance* of the self). It is probably fair to conclude that with respect to social networks, the social avatar is the unifying vehicle that delivers the dangers of social media to the door of the psyche, and can facilitate both shifts in identity and affect the psyche (in direct and indirect ways, and in multiple directions).

The time users spend considering their digital image and choosing material for the creation of a social avatar appears to vastly exceed any personal thinking time with respect to the effects this could be having on the psyche. This must be rectified, as bringing the various components of online and offline aspects of identity into one balanced, harmonious whole (i.e., closing the gap), is recognised to be beneficial, with personal integration being described as a hallmark of mental health [21]. Social media and the creation of a social avatar therefore seem unlikely to either help with this process of integration, or enhance the psychological authenticity necessary for well-being in the longer term.

There can be no doubt that social media is a hungry animal, with a swelling pack of followers. However, whilst the advantages in communication may be enjoyed by many, and there remains a *theoretical* possibility that (due to the sheer numbers of social media users alone) the average psychological nature of users will be 'normal' overall, this appears to be increasingly unlikely – and, as this chapter has considered, there is much for users to contend with and the potential pitfalls for the psyche are many.

Table 8. The Potential Dangers of Social Media for the Psyche

Social Media Aspect	Danger for the Psyche
Over-sharing and the loss of privacy	Must be lamented – everything that is lost has a purpose; as if it didn't, it wouldn't exist as human need in the first place (perhaps privacy is necessary for creativity, or to allow rejuvenation for example)
The problem of narcissism	Narcissists behave online as they do offline, i.e., social media is fuel, and its opportunities for self-promotion nourish and assist in the regulation of narcissistic esteem. But how does this affect the masses – does it effectively confer a pressure to conform to everyone else's narcissistic social avatar?
The creation of social avatars	Social avatars are created and self-rendered by users of social media in an unthinking fashion, and mostly without realising that they are effectively facilitating a psychologically significant 'gap' between the *substance* of the self (offline) and the idealised *representation* of the self (online)
It impacts on psychological authenticity	It is hard to see how social media enhances psychological authenticity (which plays a key role in healthy psychological functioning and subjective well-being). It probably inhibits it at best, and damages it at worst
Intertwined with celebrity worship	By sharing platforms with the rich and famous, unrealistic and unhelpful aims may be reinforced: 'few things are more destructive than a combination of high entitlement and a lazy work ethic' [44]
Can promote destructive & unhelpful emotions	Is constant and accessible comparison helpful, psychologically healthy, or even real? Envy, jealousy, and so-called 'smiling' depression may result/be maintained
Associated with changes in behaviour	There is an element of the self-fulfilling prophesy about the way we represent the self online (this is just one aspect of the digital world which should be included into a dramatically widened program of cyber-education/digital citizenship)
Can collide with real life in unexpected ways	Psychologically violent and rude awakenings and an increased need to save face have been reported in the context of 'gap' exposure in social media use – incidence unknown, but clinically significant due to destructive nature
Early exposure to traditionally adult experiences	Social media is part of this phenomenon (sometimes in a closed loop away from adult eyes). Examples such as pornographic sexting and relationship revenge postings must surely have the potential to affect development, worldview and tenable relationship behaviour in the longer term?

Table 8. (Continued)

Social Media Aspect	Danger for the Psyche
Forms much of the modern substrate for identity formation	The online world is becoming *the* social cultural aspect to identity formation. Does it assist, or hinder, in the achievement of a stable identity?
Promotes multi-tasking and brevity	Sometimes attending to less has more value. Loss of context can also be bewildering - in the spirit of this observation, enough said
Sustains/encourages the utilisation of (unhelpful) defence mechanisms	Projection, rationalisation, intellectualisation, compartmentalization, denial, distortion and other self-preserving cognitive biases - all can be identified on analysis
Can take over in unexpected ways	For the vulnerable (? few), self-promotion can take over self-awareness to the extent that it is suspected and reported that individuals are beginning to value cyberspace over reality
Can host cyberbullying	A straight-forward example of social media representing dangers to the psyche of those involved
May be part of problematic internet use (PIU)	Focus has been on gaming to date, but with over a billion users of social networks, this focus appears too narrow, and is also a diversion from the need to develop a fuller, richer awareness and understanding
The problem of permanence	We are not built to remember everything and be reminded of everything for good reason
May host the 'E-Personality'	Disinhibited and disassociated, the e-personality is thought to develop when normal (offline) rules are discarded, and the darker side of human nature can surface [5]. This identity shift may be implicated in some of the more antisocial online behaviour
Can host antisocial online behaviours	Trolling, revenge postings of a sexual nature, obituary defacement etc. are other illustrative examples with direct implications for the psyche of those involved
To be announced (T.B.A.)	This summary is not exhaustive. Perhaps it will continue to evolve in line with technology updates, ubiquitous uptake and human nature itself?

Such is its appetite for content, and coupled with the user's thirst for self-promotion, this chapter has considered and highlighted the notion that social media can insidiously appropriate things which should really be protected. Indeed, for many (unthinking) users, potential losses such as authenticity and privacy do not appear to be being noticed (and even if they are, may be deemed a price worth paying to the piper?)

But what is a world without previously valued experiences like authenticity, privacy and a sense of modesty? It seems that for every successful long term celebrity, there is another on the psychological scrap heap, and there is therefore an urgent need to get the blinkers off, and to recognise the duality which exists within our use of social media (good for us/bad for us).

The final table of this chapter (Table 8), therefore attempts to summarise the psychological concerns or 'dangers' with respect to social media and their potential to affect the psyche (it is not considered exhaustive, is in no particular order, and represents the author's consideration). It also now appears that the relationship between social media and the psyche is not only complicated by the sheer number of influential psychological aspects at play, but by the bi-directional nature of these influences as well. For example, the research into the relationships between narcissism and social media considered in this chapter clearly demonstrate that personality aspects can have an online manifestation (i.e., a *forwards* direction). Alternatively, this chapter has also demonstrated the erosive effects of social media upon psychological authenticity via the social avatar (i.e., a *backwards* direction).

Table 8 is therefore a fitting conclusion to this chapter's contention: That social media *does* present dangers to the psyche, and if left un-checked, we would do well to remember that 'modern man does not feel happy with his god-like nature' [57].

Author's Note

One of the most interesting things about writing this chapter has been the myriad of information to consider and the different viewpoints which are available online and otherwise. This chapter has, for example, contended that psychological authenticity is an insidious and inevitable sacrifice for using social media. The author duly notes however, that others may develop more optimistic viewpoints, such as 'there are the beginnings of a reinforcement process happening online, in which people are being rewarded for being more real' [58]. In the same vein, it is also acknowledged that the chapter has focussed exclusively on the potential dangers of social media (to/for the psyche). This chapter does not intend to be a polemic; it simply prefers to trust others will continue to promote the many and undoubted virtues of social media and the internet, as enjoyed by many. In this sense, the chapter may also be criticised as 'part of the problem in an at times polarising, unclear and sensationalist commentary and debate' [35]. However, readers can be assured that it represents an honest attempt to shine a psychological torch into a murky area. It is hoped that, at the very least, this chapter offers a brief evaluation of where we might be in this great, exciting and ultimately risky experiment with the psyche; although if it causes some to pause, reflect on where we are heading and what we might lose on the way there, that will do nicely too.

The author reports no conflict of interest. The author alone is responsible for the content and writing of the chapter. An earlier, shorter version of this chapter (approximately 35% content) was published in the December 2013 issue of Australasian Psychiatry, under the title of:

Social media, social avatars and the psyche: Is Facebook good for us? DOI: 10.1177/1039856213509289.

REFERENCES

[1] Te Kaunihera Tapuhi o Aotearoa/Nursing Council of New Zealand (2013) *Social Media and Electronic Communication Guidelines* http://www.nursingcouncil.org.nz/download/309/smedia.pdf (Accessed 19 April 2013).

[2] Kiss, J. (2012) 'Facebook hits 1 billion users per month' http://www.guardian.co.uk/technology/2012/oct/04/facebook-hits-billion-users-a-month (Accessed 19 April 2013).

[3] Aboujaoude, E. (2010) Problematic Internet Use: An Overview *World Psychiatry* 2010; 9:85 – 90/.

[4] Mehdizadeh, S. (2010) Self Presentation 2.0: Narcissism and Self-Esteem on Facebook *Cyberpsychology, Behaviour and Social Networking*. Volume 13, Number 4, 2010.

[5] Aboujaoude, E. (2011) *Virtually You – The Dangerous Powers of the E-Personality* First Edition, 2011 W.W.Norton & Company, New York.

[6] Penguin Family Dictionary (2006) Penguin Books, 2006 Edition, London.

[7] Cohn, M. (2010) 'The importance of having a face on the internet' Created on 5 June 2010 http://www.compukol.com/blog/the-importance-of-having-a-face-on-the-internet/ (Accessed 19 April 2013).

[8] Sunstrum, K. (2014) 'How Social Media Affects Our Self-Perception' Psych central http://psychcentral.com/blog/archives/2014/03/14/how-social-media-affects-our-self-perception/ (Accessed on September 3, 2014).

[9] The Australian Medical Association Council of Doctors-in-Training (2013) The New Zealand Medical Association Doctors-in-Training Council (2013) The New Zealand Medical Students' Association (2013) The Australian Medical Students' Association (2103) *Social Media and the Medical Profession: A guide to online professionalism for medical practitioners and medical students* http://www.nzmsa.org.nz/resources/ social-media-guide/ (Accessed 19 April 2013).

[10] Frankish, K et al. (2012) Psychiatry and Online Social Media: Potential, pitfalls and ethical guidelines for psychiatrists and trainees *Australasian Psychiatry* 2012; 20(3): 181 – 187.

[11] Mansfield, S et al. (2011) Social Media and the Medical Profession *Medical Journal of Australia* 2011; 194 (12): 642-644.

[12] Anderson, T. (2013) 'Engage, don't broadcast: the need for authenticity in social media' http://www.theguardian.com/technology/ 2013/aug/12 /engage-dont-broadcast-the-need-for-authenticity-in-social-media (Accessed 20 August, 2014).

[13] Neate, P. (2009) *Jerusalem* Published in Penguin Books, 2010.

[14] Fields, J (2011-2013) 'Is Social Media Killing Authenticity?' http://www.jonathanfields.com/is-social-media-killing-authenticity/ (Accessed 20 August, 2014).

[15] Maslow, A.H. (1968) *Toward a psychology of being* 2nd Edition, Princeton, NJ: Van Nostrand.

[16] Rogers, C. (1961) *On becoming a person: A therapists view of Psychotherapy* Boston: Houghton Mifflin.

[17] Goldman, B.M. and Kernis, M.H. (2002) The role of authenticity in healthy psychological functioning and subjective well-being *Annals of the American Psychotherapy Association* Nov-Dec 2002, Volume 5, Issue 6, p18-20.

[18] Fawn, M. (2011) Living Authentically with Mental Depression http://health.wikinut.com/Living-Authentically-with-Mental-Depression/dyclhtj1/ (Accessed 20 August, 2014).

[19] Banks, J. (2014) *5 Minutes with Banks* M2woman.co.nz Sep/Oct 2014, p.32.

[20] Preston, A. (2014) 'The death of privacy' www.theguardian.com http://www.theguardian.com/world/2014/aug/03/internet-death-privacy-google-facebook-alex-preston (Accessed 20 August, 2014).

[21] Suler, J. (2001) The Online Disinhibition Effect The Psychology of Cyberspace – The Classic Text (January 1996 – Present Day)

http://users.rider.edu/~suler/psycyber/disinhibit.html (Accessed 4 September, 2014).

[22] Schwartz, B.M. (2003) 'Hot or Not? Website Briefly Judges Looks' The Harvard Crimson, November 4, 2003 http://www.thecrimson.com/ article/2003/11/4/hot-or-not-website-briefly-judges/.

[23] Suler, J. (1996) Identity Management in Cyberspace The Psychology of Cyberspace – The Classic Text (January 1996 – Present Day) http://users.rider.edu/~suler/psycyber/identitymanage.html (Accessed 4 September, 2014).

[24] Suler, J (1998) Personality Types in Cyberspace The Psychology of Cyberspace – The Classic Text (January 1996 – Present Day) http://users.rider.edu/~suler/psycyber/persontypes.html (Accessed 4 September, 2014).

[25] Brunskill, D. (2013) Social media, social avatars and the psyche: Is Facebook good for us? *Australasian Psychiatry*, December 2013; 21(6): 527-532.

[26] Suler, J. (1999) Avatar Psychotherapy The Psychology of Cyberspace – The Classic Text (January 1996 – Present Day) http://users.rider.edu/ ~suler/psycyber/avatarther.html (Accessed 4 September, 2014).

[27] Brunskill, D. (2013) Social avatar – in 100 words *The British Journal of Psychiatry,* 2013; 203:386.

[28] Noll et al. (2009) Childhood Abuse, Avatar Choices, and Other risk factors Associated With Internet-Initiated Victimization of Adolescent girls *Paediatrics.* June 2009; 123(6): e1078-e1083. Doi:10.1542 /peds.2008-2983.

[29] Yee, N and Bailenson, J. (2007) The Proteus Effect: the effect of transformed self-representation on behaviour. *Hum. Commun Res.*, 2007; 33(3): 271-290.

[30] Katene-Hill, H (2014) '25 Worst Things About Social Media' M2magazine.co.nz April 2014, Issue 107: 40-43.

[31] Galletly, C. A. (2010) Ask patients about their internet use Letters to the *Editor Medical Journal of Australia* 2010; 193 (5): 312.

[32] Australian Psychological Society National Psychology Week Survey (2010) *The Social and Psychological Impact of Online Social Networking* http://www.psychology.org.au/Assets/Files/Social-and-Psychological-Impact-of-Social-Networking-Sites.pdf (Accessed 19 April 2013).

[33] Bostic, J.Q. and Brunt, C. C. (2011) Cornered: An Approach to School Bullying and Cyberbullying, and Forensic Implications *Child and*

Adolescent Psychiatric Clinics of North America: 2011; Volume 20: 447-465. Doi:10.1016/j.chc.2011.03.004.

[34] Diagnostic and Statistical Manual of Mental Disorders (DSM-5, 2013) Fifth Edition, 2013 American Psychiatric Association.

[35] Tam, P and Walter, G. (2014) Problematic internet use in childhood and youth: evolution of a 21st century affliction *Australasian Psychiatry*, Volume 21, Number 6, December 2014, 533-536.

[36] Campbell's Psychiatric Dictionary (2009) 9th Edition Oxford University Press, 2009.

[37] Brunskill, D. (2012) *Saving Face* Presented at Hong Kong Academy of Medicine Faculty of Forensic Psychiatry Conference The Civil and Criminal Aspects of Memory and Dissociation The Royal Australian and New Zealand College of Psychiatrists Hong Kong: 4-7th September, 2012.

[38] Gabbard, G. (2012) Clinical challenges in the internet era *The American Journal of Psychiatry* 2012; 169 (5): 460 – 463.

[39] Dokoupil, T. (2012) 'Is the Web Driving Us Mad?' http://www. thedailybeast.com/newsweek/2012/07/08/is-the-internet-making-us-crazy- what-the-new-research-says.html. (Created on 9 July 2012, Accessed on 19 June 2013)

[40] Twenge, J.M. and Campbell, K.W. (2008, 2009) About *The Narcissism Epidemic*: An FAQ on narcissism www.narcissismepidemic. com http://www.narcissismepidemic.com/aboutbook.html (Accessed 20 August, 2014)

[41] Buffardi, L.E. and Campbell, K.W. (2008) Narcissism and Social Networking Websites *Pers Soc Psychol Bull* October 2008 vol. 34 no. 10 1303-1314

[42] Oxford Dictionaries Press Release (2013) www.oxforddictionaries.com http://blog.oxforddictionaries.com/press-releases/oxford-dictionaries-word-of-the-year-2013 (Accessed 20 August, 2014)

[43] Freedland, J. (2013) 'The selfie's screaming narcissism masks an urge to connect'http://www.theguardian.com/commentisfree/2013/nov/19/selfie-narcissism-oxford-dictionary-word (Accessed 20 August, 2014)

[44] Chamorro-Premusik, T. (March 2014) 'Sharing the (self) love: the rise of the selfie and digital narcissism' www.theguardian.com http://www. theguardian.com/media-network/media-network-blog/2014/mar/13/selfie-social-media-love-digital-narcassism (Accessed 20 August, 2014).

[45] Chamorro-Premusik, T. (August 2014) 'Kim Kardashian: why we love her and the psychology of celebrity worship' www.theguardian.com http://www.theguardian.com/media-network/media-network-blog/2014/aug/14/kim-kardashian-psychology-celebrity-worship-social-media (Accessed 20 August, 2014).

[46] Uhls, Y.T. and Greenfield, P. M. (2012) The Value of Fame: Preadolescent Perceptions of Popular Media and Their Relationship to Future Aspirations *Developmental Psychology*, 2012. March; 48 (2):315-26. doi: 10.1037/a0026369

[47] Jayson, S. (2013) 'Survey: Young people who use social media seek fame' http://www.usatoday.com/story/news/nation/2013/04/18/social-media-tweens-fame/2091199/ (Accessed 20 August, 2014)

[48] Wood, M. (2014) 'How Young Is Too Young for a Digital Presence?' www.nytimes.com http://www.nytimes.com/2014/05/15/technology/personaltech/how-young-is-too-young-for-a-digital-presence.html?_r=0 (Accessed 20 August, 2014)

[49] Erikson, E. (1950) *Childhood and Society* Chapter 6: Toys and Reasons W.W. Norton & Company; Reissue edition (September 17, 1993)

[50] Shaffer, D.R and Kipp, K. (2009) *Developmental Psychology: Childhood and Adolescence* Chapter 12: Development of the Self and Social cognition. 8th Edition, Wadsworth Publishing (January 13, 2009)

[51] Marcia, J.E. (1966) Development and validation of ego identity status *J. Personal. Soc. Psychol.* 3:551-558, 1966.

[52] Uhls, Y.T., & Greenfield, P.M. (2011) The Rise of Fame: An Historical Content Analysis. *Cyberpsychology: Journal of Psychosocial Research on Cyberspace, 5*(1), article 1. http://cyberpsychology.eu/ view.php ?cisloclanku=2011061601&article=1 (Accessed 20 August, 2014)

[53] Cohen, J. (2014) *Interview material quoted in Preston*, A. (2014) 'The death of privacy' www.theguardian.com http://www.theguardian.com/world/2014/aug/03/internet-death-privacy-google-facebook-alex-preston (Accessed 20 August, 2014)

[54] Luft, J. and Ingham, H. (1955) *The Johari window, a graphic model of interpersonal awareness* Proceedings of the western training laboratory in group development Los Angeles: UCLA, 1955

[55] Lopez De Victoria, S. (2008). 'The Johari Window' www.psychcentral.com http://psychcentral.com/blog/archives/2008/07/08/the-johari-window/(Retrieved 20 August, 2014)

[56] Simba. (2010) In response to 'Is Social Media Killing Authenticity by Field, J. June 10, 2010 at 11:58 am http://www.jonathanfields.com/is-social-media-killing-authenticity/ (Accessed 20 August, 2014)
[57] Freud, S. (1930) *Civilization and its Discontents* Classic Edition, 2002 Penguin Books, London.
[58] Suler, J. (2014) On Authenticity *Personal Electronic Communication*, 2014.

In: Social Media
Editor: Annmarie Bennet

ISBN: 978-1-63463-175-4
© 2015 Nova Science Publishers, Inc.

Chapter 5

THE *MATRIX* HERO ON YOUTUBE: FAN VIDS AS A FORM OF TRANSMEDIA STORYTELLING

Dorothy Wai-sim Lau
Academy of Film, Hong Kong Baptist University, Hong Kong

ABSTRACT

Fan vids are an emergent form of storytelling in the current social media epoch. As a genre of works, they comprise montages of visual material culled [*]from mass media source texts and set to music through the grassroots practice of vidding. As vidders search, cull, and edit movie images, they recast the cinematic stories by decontextualizing the source materials and extending the frontier of the narrative to other signifying realms. Vidding could be said to constitute a grassroots, fan-driven form of transmedia storytelling, by which the integral elements of a fiction are systematically dispersed across multiple media platforms. *The Matrix*, a celebrated Hollywood science fiction franchise, has inspired many such instances of transmedia storytelling, demonstrating how the story is retold by ordinary fans as they transpose movie images from cinematic space to cyberspace. This essay focuses on two fan vids from YouTube, the most popular video-sharing site, entitled "I, Neo (Mos Def / Massive Attack / Matrix Mashup)" and "Matrix Vs. Excision & Downlink - Existence VIP Dub Mashup" to examine how vidders incorporate new content to expand and alter the *Matrix* narrative into the bottom-up generated content. When *Matrix* footage is eclectically cut to electronic music, Neo's story is no

[*] dorolau@hkbu.edu.hk.

longer represented and understood within a fixed symbolic system, but rather in a hybrid, open framework, allowing for diverse directionality of interpretation. While transmedia storytelling conventions stress that all components from all media should cohere with a consistent narrative world, *The Matrix* story in these fan vids is embellished by insinuating a narrative rupture. The vids allow a narrative experience which is fragmented, inconsistent, or even disintegrated, partaking of a postmodernist discourse. Although *The Matrix*'s original allusions to messianic-redemptive Christian mythology, of particular interest for my analysis, remain apparent in these vids, the vidders have obscured, altered, and reworked the cinematic story, concomitantly generating new stories. Fan vids open up new possibilities for re-presenting and re-interpreting media texts, posing both challenges and opportunities for the practices of storytelling and meaning-making in the global mediascape.

Keywords: Social media, fan vid, storytelling, transmedia, participatory

INTRODUCTION: STORYTELLING IN THE USER-GENERATED MEDIASCAPE

Fan vids are an emergent vehicle for storytelling within the social media landscape. An "underground art form" (Russo 2009), fan vids are montages of visual material culled from mass media source texts and set to music through the practice of vidding. They are the creative output of the media audiences, Internet users empowered by the prevalent availability of high bandwidth and free video-editing software.[1] One particularly popular genre of fan vids is the mashup, a term denoting a "remix" of digital data, in which discretely sourced images and sounds are edited together to form a novel composite video. Known for their diversification of approaches to their subject matter (Jenkins 2006b), vidders celebrate, critique, and parody cultural texts, filtering their source images through a web of intertextual signification. They pair music with pre-existing visual materials dislodged from their original interpretive

[1] The music video "Closer," made by T. Jonesy and Killa using footage from *Star Trek, can be said to be one of the first Internet fan vids*. As Jake Coyle (2008) has argued, Jonesy and Killa used *Star Trek* to reimagine rk Romanek's original video for the industrial rock group Nine Inch Nails, chiefly by recasting Kirk and Spock's relationship in homoerotic innuendo. Widely circulated in the blogosphere during fall 2006, this slash vid was hyped as grassroots art facilitated by digital image-making technology.

backgrounds to stage readings of their "new stories," (Coppa 2008),[2] employing the music as an interpretive lens allowing viewers to discern and construe the visuals differently. Fan vids thus offer a visual-sonic space for alternative modes of meaning-making in relation to cinematic images.

As a genre, fan vids reflect the dramatic transformation of movie fandom by recent advances in technology. Vidding began in mid-1970s with amateur use of slide projector stills, grew through the 1980s and 1990s with the development of VHS and DVD technology, and by the 2000s attained near-universal feasibility via the Internet. (Russo 2009) A proliferation of fan sites now allows audiences to post and circulate news and stories of their idols with remarkable speed and spread, and since the mid-2000s, the maturation of broadband infrastructure and image-making software have made cinematic texts promptly available for fans' appropriation and manipulation. Through the common formats of QuickTime streaming and Flash animation, video files are now downloadable and directly transferable between the devices such as television and computer. Cinephiles can now easily search, cull, copy, and share movie stills, trailers, and clips from digital sources like DVDs and Internet websites. In addition to the appropriation of texts, they can also edit these images and hybridize them with other texts using digital image-making technology. Like other artists, vidders are known for their sophisticated and intelligent use of appropriated materials in telling their own versions of stories (Jenkins 2006b); moreover, they eagerly post and share their work on video-sharing sites, soliciting support or feedback from the fanvid community. While following in the tradition of older fan-oriented productions like fanzines,[3] fan vids advance the genre of fan writing by facilitating bottom-up generated content, unlike the works of fanzine writers and editors, who are often leading members in the fan communities. Fan vids thus constitute a democratized form of media production, lengthening the reach of fan activity and transforming the nature of fandom in an era of user-generated media.

The digitalization of media facilitates a different approach to sharing, interpreting and re-telling Hollywood narratives. Classical Hollywood cinema has cultivated "a sturdy and pervasive tradition of storytelling." (Bordwell 2007) Dating to the 1920s and 1930s, this tradition has become a filmmaking

[2] Coppa further points out the error of Coyle's assumption that fans who make music videos are necessarily fans of the music itself, as suggested by his recent news article, "The Best Fan-Made Music Videos on YouTube."

[3] Fanzines, along with self-published slash fiction, originated in the 1930s and became popular during the 1940s (Wikipedia: Fanzine). They represent earlier modes of grassroots fan-created works, in contrast to the top-down modes of film and star promotion through professional journalism and studio propaganda.

style against which many others are judged. As David Bordwell observes in his seminal book *The Classical Hollywood Cinema* (1985), classical Hollywood narrative films feature plots which progress in a linear fashion, dependent on character-driven action and the use of continuity editing. Simple and clear, their plots abjure excessive details and draw upon basic principles of classical literature to achieve a balance and symmetry in which all components are integrated into a diegetic whole. Narrative time and space are further unified and aligned with perception of reality through the use of techniques like eye-line match, the 180-degree rule, and point-of-view shots. Such techniques allow the viewer to "suspend disbelief," convincing us that what we see on the screen is true. As John Belton (2006) explains, "Classical Hollywood cinema possesses a style which is largely invisible and difficult for the average spectator to see. The narrative is delivered so effortlessly and efficiently to the audience that it appears to have no source. It comes magically off the screen." (22)[4] The resulting sense of harmony satisfies and even exhilarates the audience.

While fan vids often employ footage from acclaimed Hollywood movies, the classical narrative style itself is rarely retained. As vidders cut movie footage to music and move it from the cinematic context to the new media context, they retell the stories in novel ways, exhibiting a fan-driven, bottom-up generated form of transmedia storytelling. "Transmedia," as writer-designer-researcher Christy Dena observes, has become a buzzword in recent years (TMSB, 2012), denoting a theoretical model for considering the flow of content across media. "Transmedia storytelling," a term popularized by Henry Jenkins (2011), signifies a process by which integral elements of a fiction are systematically dispersed across multiple media platforms for the purpose of creating a coordinated and cohesive entertainment experience. This process by nature enhances fan participation since, as Jenkins (2006a) puts it, consumers in an age of media convergence can meld together multiple texts to create a larger narrative than could be contained in a single medium. (95) This idea is echoed by Marc Ruppel (2006), who elaborates on "cross-sited narratives," new structures that "shatter the fixity of narrative as a single-medium endeavor and establish instead a multiply-mediated storyworld." (185) Narrative theorist Jill Walker (2004) also explores the notion of "distributed narratives," which take further the postmodern narratives illustrating "fragments and bricolage in content, plot, and style". (1) This "emergent form" (100) "open[s] up the

[4] John Belton calls this style the driving force of the "narrative machine," hinting the industrial mode of moviemaking.

formal and physical aspects of the work and spread[s itself] across time, space and the network." (1)[5] Similarly, Glorianna Davenport has described the "very distributed stories" (Davenport et al. 2000), made possible by the expanded role of the media audience. These stories are the "narratives of the future [that] are capable of expanding the social engagement of audiences while offering intensive narrative immersion in a story experience that plays out in multiple public and private venues." (Ibid.) Transmedia stories rely not on individual characters or specific plotline, but on a larger fictional composite which can sustain manifold interconnected characters and their stories. The creative process is cumulative: storytellers add details like character backstories and secondary plotline to the composite fiction, aggrandizing the power of the story in scope and significance.

The participatory attributes of transmedia storytelling complement those of social media, enabling the audience to actively participate in the creation or re-creation of the narrative. By so doing, they become social and creative collaborators; they become, in Rutledge's terms, the "stakeholders" of the transmedia experience (Rutledge). The paradigm of the "never-final" story motivates the audience to seek out untold parts of the narrative and extend it by adding content, illustrating what Henry Jenkins (2011) calls extension in contrast to adaptation: while both involve shifts between media, adaptation fundamentally takes the same story from one medium and retells it in another whereas extension adds new content to the narrative as it moves from one medium to another.[6] Extension facilitates what game designer Neil Young terms "additive comprehension," whereby the addition of a small segment may alter the entire perception of the film. (Jenkins 2006a: 123) By de-/re-contextualizing cinematic materials, vidders extend the narrative boundary, transforming fans' intended participation in retelling the story. They also engage with other fan participants, exhibiting a highly interactive storytelling process. When vidders upload their works on online video-sharing sites, they invite other users in the same network to "like," comment on, and share them, producing a seamless and instantaneous interaction among users. These

[5] The notion of "distribution" designates a lack of unity which can be elaborated into three aspects: distribution in time – the narrative cannot be experienced in one consecutive period of time; second, distribution in space -- no single place in which the whole narrative can be experienced; third, distribution of authorship -- no single author or group of authors can have complete control over the form of the narrative. (Walker 2004: 3)

[6] Christy Dena has challenged this view of Jenkins, arguing that adaptation can also be profoundly transformative instead of being merely literal. Any adaptations, to a certain extent, add something new to the array of meanings attached to the stories. As Dena points out, shifts between media imply new experiences and new lessons. (Jenkins 2011)

participatory acts by various users accumulate, connect, and work together to effect a multifaceted, versatile story and cross-media entertainment experience. The endless appropriation, reproduction, and circulation of movie images remaps the practice of storytelling in a networked entertainment landscape, demonstrating an unprecedented degree of participation and interactivity among audiences.

RETELLING THE *MATRIX* STORY

The Matrix, a celebrated 1999 Hollywood movie, is an influential example of transmedia storytelling (Jenkins 2006a: 101) frequently sourced on video-sharing sites. Like other vast entertainment networks, Hollywood has the potential to realize innovative transmedia projects (Dena), and *The Matrix* in particular has developed into an unprecedented cyberpunk science-fiction phenomenon. Produced by Warner Bros., the film was the highest-grossing R-rated film of 1999 in North America, and has since been acknowledged as "the most influential action movie of the generation" (Fierman 2003). The *Matrix* franchise, extended by two sequels, three video games, comic books, and a collection of animated stories, successfully established a cult following whose members are fascinated not only by the captivating action, but also by the compelling story and philosophical underpinnings. Particularly famous scenes relevant to the plot development, such as the "I know kung fu" scene from *The Matrix* and the "Neo-versus-multiple-Smiths" scene from *The Matrix Reloaded* are much-recalled and discussed. Because the narrative taps into a discourse sustained by myriad cultural and media elements, viewers are unlikely to read it from a single perspective – an effect intended by its original creators, Lana and Andy Wachowski, who explicitly sought to juxtapose elements from various cultures in a ground-breaking manners. (Jenkins 2006: 121) This narrative eclecticism is underscored and expanded in the user-generated fan texts collaboratively reworked in the Web-based environment.

This essay will consider *The Matrix* as an exemplary case for observing how a narrative evolves when transposed from cinematic space to cyberspace. I have chosen YouTube as the primary site of investigation, as it is among the most popular video-sharing sites, with more than 1 billion user visits and 6 billion hours of video-viewing each month. (YouTube Statistics) Many video clips sourcing *The Matrix* are in circulation on YouTube; I keyword-searched the site by using the phrase "Matrix, mashup" to identify the most-viewed clips of that genre. The top 20 results (out of 69,400 as of April 12, 2014) consisted primarily of two types: mashups of *The Matrix* with another film[7] and fan vids featuring *Matrix* footage cut to music. I have chosen to concentrate on the latter type, for the purpose of exploring fan vids' capacity for wedding disparate visual and sonic elements. Two fan vids, "I, Neo (Mos Def / Massive Attack / Matrix Mashup)" and "Matrix Vs. Excision & Downlink - Existence VIP Dub Mashup" will serve as texts for analysis.

While transmedia storytelling as conventionally understood entails a coherent and coordinated development of the story-world through each new medium, in these fan vids the story of *The Matrix* is embellished by insinuating a narrative rupture, thus providing a narrative experience which is fragmented, inconsistent, or even disintegrated, partaking of a postmodernist discourse. Although certain themes from the original cinematic materials remain apparent in the fan vids, the vidders have obscured, altered, and reworked Neo's story as they hybridize *Matrix* footage with electronic music. The vids thereby open up new signifying possibilities, enabling fans as collaborative agents to create new stories in the post-cinematic epoch.

STORYTELLING, MYTHOLOGY, AND MEANING MAKING IN *THE MATRIX*

Storytelling always entails a myth-making process. Christopher Vogler, a writing teacher as well as a student of famous mythologist Joseph Campbell, explains the nature of myth in his book *The Writer's Journey* (1992):

> "What is a myth? For our purposes a myth is not the untruth or fanciful exaggeration of popular expression. A myth, as Campbell was fond of saying, is a metaphor for a mystery beyond human comprehension. It is a comparison that helps us understand, by analogy, some aspect of our mysterious selves. A myth, in this way of thinking, is not an untruth but a way of reaching a profound truth. Then what is a story? A story is also a metaphor, a model of some aspect of human behavior." (p. vii)

The myth-making process has characterized Hollywood production from the classical era to the contemporary era. The archetypal "heroes," abstracted from mythological sources, are incarnated through a range of characters from

[7] The films that YouTube users cut to juxtapose with *The Matrix* include *Inception* (2010), *Watchmen* (2009), *The Dark Knight* (2008), *Fight Club* (1999), and *Kung Fu Panda* (2008), all Hollywood productions with thematic or generic proximity to *The Matrix*.

cowboys to comic-book heroes, all immediately recognizable to audiences. The "hero's journey," as conceptualized by Campbell prescribes a sequence of tasks the protagonist must complete while undergoing a corporeal and spiritual ordeal. Stories of the Western genre, for example, convey values such as rugged individualism, justice, pioneering spirit, and courage, incarnated by a lone hero who triumphs over the outlaws, embodying a warrior code of honor in a world threatened by moral breakdown. The superhero genre adapts familiar comic book narratives of folklore heroes (*Superman*, *Batman*, *The Fantastic Four*, *X-Men*), who protect the promise of the well-ordered American society from villains seeking to subvert it, through a salvific struggle that evokes the eternal conflict between good and evil. *Superman*, specifically, is in Mark Stucky's (2006) phrase the "popular culture's paradigmatic hero," whose humanity both conceals and makes possible his supernatural destiny evoking the figure of Christ. In the movie version of *Superman*, the narrative cycle relays of a complex calling involving three distinct tasks and journeys: first, to go to and live among Earth's people; second, to withdraw from Earth's people; and third, to save Earth's people. (Stucky 2006) Each of the three missions directs the hero toward an eventual symbolic death and resurrection, followed by the experience of atonement. By evoking Christian mythology, *Superman*'s narrative cycle also reconnects audiences with the older works in our culture, concomitantly giving those works new currency.

Like *Superman*, *The Matrix* also borrows substantially from the mythological sources of the Christian faith. While *The Matrix* narrative references a wide array of religious and philosophical systems, including Buddhism, science-fiction ontological theories of the Philip K. Dick school, Taoism, martial-arts mysticism, and Godelian mathematical metaphysics. Christianity is probably the most familiar. The Christian undertones are readily evident in the use of biblical names and a plot revolving around the Redeemer myth. Neo (Keanu Reeves), whose surname "Anderson" means "son of man," is the chosen "One," analogous to the Christ. In a world where humans are enslaved from birth by the unseen but all-controlling Matrix, Neo is hailed as the one to free them, similar to Christ's prophesized arrival to free humans from the blind slavery of sin hereditary to everyone born from Adam.[8] The liberation-through-enlightenment from the Matrix enables people to be born anew from their life support pods, seeing the universal oppression encircling them from a new perspective, similar to the spiritual rebirth Christians gain

---

[8] Reference to chapter 5 of the Book of Romans in the Bible.

from conversion.[9] After escaping from the illusions of the Matrix, the liberated reside in the city of Zion, a reference to the city of the Promised Land (Jerusalem) in the Old Testament, ad perhaps also to the Christian Church, called "daughter of Zion" in the New Testament. Morpheus (Laurence Fishburne), who identifies Neo as the One, brings to mind, John the Baptist, who heralds the coming of "the Chosen One" in the wilderness; his ship, the hovercraft Nebuchadnezzar, has the same name as the biblical Babylonian king whose prophetic dreams could only be interpreted by Daniel. Neo and his comrades are betrayed by their fellow Cypher – as Jesus was by Judas, one of the twelve disciples – upon which Neo gives his life to save Morpheus, reinforcing the messianic connotation. After death, he is resurrected by the kiss, or breath, of Trinity, akin to the Holy Spirit, and defeats the sinister Agent Smith using his newfound mastery over the Matrix. As the movie closes, Neo ascends into the clouds, having declared a new mission to free those still in bondage to the Matrix. The abundant biblical references in *The Matrix* evince a strong influence from the myths of the Christian culture informing its narrative.

NEO ON YOUTUBE

The Christian themes prominent *The Matrix* narrative attenuate when vidders cull passages from the film and transpose them from the cinema screen to the computer screen, "mashing" them with other media. Viewers read the classical redemptive myths through a new lens as biblical motifs merge with those from other texts. A fan vid uploaded March 8, 2007 on YouTube entitled "I, Neo (Mos Def / Massive Attack / Matrix Mashup)" offers one such example. User "garrisonmedia" has cut clips from *The Matrix Revolutions* (2003), the last installment of *The Matrix* trilogy, to the song "I against I," performed by *Mos Def* and Massive Attack. The footage proceeds from Neo's vantage point of view, drawing on the "Neo-versus-Smith" scene, a battle set in a futuristic urban milieu. Near its beginning, the video depicts the combat between the hero and the villain on a rainy night. The fight seems prolonged, extending from one locale to another – from outdoor to indoor, from the ground to the air. Audiences see the thrusts, leaps and kicks of the two fighters, augmented by both wire work and the computer-generated special effects.

[9] Reference to chapter 3 of the Book of John in the Bible.

The song "I against I" dominates the sonic space of the video, with the occasional inclusion of dialogue between Neo and Smith heard over the music. The lyrics, in part, proclaim:

> ya,
> I against I,
> Flesh of my flesh,
> And mind of my mind,
> Two of a kind but one won't survive,
> My images reflect in the enemies eye,
> And his images reflect in mine the same time,
>   ya, I-ya,
> I against I,
> Flesh of my flesh,
> And mind of my mind,
> Two of a kind but one won't survive,
>   Right here is where the end gon' start at,
> Conflict, Contact, Combat,
> Fighters stand where the land is marked at,
> Settle the dispute about who the livest,
> 3 word answer,
> Whoever survive this,
> Only one of us can ride forever,
> So you and I can't ride together,
> Can't live or can't die together,
> All we can do is collide together,
> So I skillfully apply the pressure,
> Won't stop until I'm forever... One!

At its best, a fan vid complicates a narrative by altering some aspect of the source material to suggest how the vidder reads the story. "I, Neo" incorporates the song "I against I," a 2002 collaboration between British trip hop group Massive Attack and the American rapper Mos Def. The lyrics complement the visual theme of battle, in light of which the phrase "I against I" could be interpreted multiple ways. Psychologically, it could suggest a schizophrenic and conflicted self-struggling to achieve an integrated ego; the vidder uses the Neo-Smith battle to suggest that the true battle happens within and can be as vigorous and violent as the battle against an evil Other. Spiritually, it presumably alludes to the well-known Rastafarian expression, "I and I,"[10] which Rastafarians use interchangeably with "we" to evoke the union of the speaker, the audience, and God. "Iya" is also a Rastafarian expression, signifying both "my friend" ad the "higher" reality.[11] The vid thus suggests a twofold inner meaning for the Neo-Smith battle: a fatal rupture within the self paradoxically making it "forever... One!" on the one hand, and a rupture between self and God leading to a realization of God-in-self on the other, blending Rastafarian mysticism with the Redeemer-hero-myth.

"I against I" was originally recorded for the soundtrack of the 2002 American vampire superhero movie, *Blade II*, and more YouTube users compliment "I, Neo's" vidder by opining that the song works as well or better with his chosen *Matrix* footage as it did in its original setting. *Blade II*, starring the Hollywood actor and martial artist Wesley Snipes, is part of a trilogy cinematizing the comic book hero, Blade, a half-vampire, half-mortal "daywalker" who protects humanity from the ravages of a vampire community preying on humans and each other. With "I, Neo," the vidder has displaced the song from one filmic context to another, to the pleasure of many viewers. Commenter "Lio Perez" enthuses, "you did a really good job you made me think that this song should have been on this soundtrack instead of blade 2 i am truly impressed the lyrics make sense to neo and smiths hatered for each other this is the best video i seen that has been cut up for this song hands down [sic]". "AKilla9" offers: "jokes!! i like dat, almost better then the blade 2 one [sic]". "ETWarlord" writes, "Very very cool!!! Best remix of this scene I've seen so far. The song is so much cooler with this than it was in "BLADE II". Not that it didn't work for BLADE, it was just better here [sic]." Even some commenters who dislike *The Matrix* are complimentary: "I hated this movie but I loved your use of the clips with my favorite song. Good Job [sic]," writes "popothechan." "I against I" offers these viewers an intriguing new reading of *The Matrix*'s spiritual and philosophical nuances, demonstrating not only the potential of new media to extend a narrative, but also the potential of *The Matrix* itself to allow re-readings in terms of narrative, character, and theme in a diverse and vibrant manner.

The fan vid "Matrix Vs. Excision & Downlink – Existence VIP Dub Mashup," uploaded on YouTube on June 28, 2011, similarly complicates the movie's narrative ties to Christian mythology. Vidder "DubifyThis" cuts

---

[10] Rastafarianism is an African-based spiritual movement which arose in Jamaica in the 1930s. Rastafarians worship the late Ethiopian Emperor, Haile Selassie I, whom they generally regard as Jesus in his Second Advent or an incarnation of God. Outside Jamaica, Rastafarianism is best known for its cultural associations with reggae music.

[11] Wikipedia: I Against I.

footage from *The Matrix* to "Existence (VIP Mix)", the title track of a 2011 collaborative EP by Canadian dubstep DJs Excision and Downlink. The video opens with a logo of the vidder's user name, like a self-promoted brand, followed by shots of the fight scene between Neo and multiple Agent Smiths in *The Matrix Reloaded* (2003). The scene shows kung-fu-fighting Neo in his flowing robe, flying through the air and delivering blows to his enemies, establishing his superb kinetic prowess. The choreography emphasizes wire work and digitally simulated action rather than traditional kung fu, underscoring the proximity between the characters of *The Matrix* films and video game characters (Jenkins 2006: 121). The video game analogy evokes the sense of immediacy experienced by gamers, as conveyed through the game world's characters. This sense of immediacy is transferred to cyberspace and replicated, if not reinvigorated, by vidders as they engage in creative acts.

The cutting of the song "Existence" to *Matrix* footage offers a new context in which to view the Neo-Smith fight, shifting away from the hero's redemptive battle against human bondage to a darker, grimmer vision in which survival of the fittest is the only path to "redemption." The eerie, digitally-generated vocal growls:

> For too long the human race has ignored designs
> Your planet is nearing destruction
> Salvation is reserved for those who pass the tests
> If you survive, an elevated existence awaits
> Initiate phase one
> Power up the bass cannon
> Fire
> Power up the bass cannon
> Fire
> Existence

The forbiddingly unnatural voice, indifference to the fate of those who fail the "tests," and haughty promises of "an elevated existence" for those who "pass," are all reminiscent of the Architect, the enigmatic computer program who created the Matrix and expects Neo to accept his predestined role in destroying and rebooting it. The fight scene the vidder chooses to pair with this lyric ends not with Neo's triumph, but with Neo forced to retreat in the face of Smith's own growing power over the Matrix. This pairing of a grimly dystopic lyric, casting doubt on the hero's ability to save anyone but himself, with footage of a fight that ends in a draw invites an uneasy, ambivalent reading of the *Matrix* narrative. We are reminded that, while Neo's self-sacrifice opens the door to "salvation" for those trapped in the Matrix, we cannot know for certain how many will avail themselves of the chance.

The song's apocalyptic imagery also recalls the notion of the world-as-Armageddon described in Christian mythology. According to the biblical Book of Revelation, at the end of time, the Messiah will return to Earth to defeat the Antichrist and the Devil, who will encamp surrounding Jerusalem (Zion), the Holy City. The lyrics of "Existence" evoke the chaos and terror afflicting a "planet... nearing destruction" and the resort to base survival instincts geared up by "the bass cannon," a symbol of power and violence. The battle is but in "phase one," suggesting an immensely protracted fight for survival in the Armageddon scenario. "Matrix Vs. Excision & Downlink" thus draws our attention to the uncertain outcome of the battle beyond, whereas "I, Neo" drew it in a more hopeful, faith-emboldened way to the battle within.

Neo's Story Never Ends: Retelling Hollywood Narratives in the Fan-Oriented Cyber-Context

While most discussions of transmedia storytelling stress the importance of continuity, insisting that all the components cohere with a consistent narrative world, the vids examined above extend the story by introducing a narrative fissure. The concept of transmedia storytelling suggests that, ideally, each media component such as a novel, comic, video game, or film makes its own contribution to a complex narrative in such a way that the resulting fiction seems whole and fulfilling. Unlike top-down media projects, which protect the integrity of continuity at the expense of manifold perspectives and open-ended participation (Jenkins 2011), fan vids effect a break from the original meaning structure -- as from the Christian mythology, in the above cases. If a myth, as Christopher Vogler puts it, helps us to understand some dimensions of our mysterious selves, fan vids complicates that myth-making process, teasing out contradictions or similarities between the narrative components and perhaps the "mysteries" they illustrate as well. In fusing Hollywood sci-fi movies with trip hop and dubstep songs, the vids probed above evoke images of an inner spiritual battle ("I, Neo") and an unsettlingly conditional salvation ("Matrix Vs. Excision & Downlink"), complicating the Christian subtext of deliverance and eternal life in *The Matrix*. In such postmodernist approach, meanings of all signs tend to be capricious and slippery; the signifiers of fan vids are "sliding," a term used by Marsha Kinder (1991) in her discussion of transmedia texts, moving fluidly across different modes of image production and media boundaries. The aforementioned vids "experiment," in Jenkins' term, with the mythology-based narrative structure by decontextualizing the story of Neo to generate a new transmedia story and, thus, new myths.

In contemplating the potential of fan vids for refashioning stories and myths, it is necessary to distinguish between grassroots media products, such as vids, and top-down media franchising, both of which could be considered transmedia phenomena in terms of the operating logic. Franchising is a corporate structure for media production that transmits brands and icons across multiple media channels, as famously seen with *Star Wars* (1977), *Indiana Jones* (1981), and *Harry Potter* (2001). The strong profit motive underpinning transmedia storytelling is evident in its synthesis of entertainment and marketing, cultivating emotional attachments to further sales (Jenkins 2006a: 104). By contrast, bottom-up generated content such as fan vids favors creative rather than economic impulses, supplementing corporate efficacy with grassroots dynamism. Vidders are amateur media producers who appropriate and rework media sources as their creativity directs. In the absence of corporatized economic resources, they nonetheless exploit the potential of creative fluidity as they reorder, reassemble, and redirect the commercial texts using video-processing technology and the social media network. This corporate-grassroots convergence is widely evident on video-sharing sites like YouTube (Burgess and Green 2009), where projects like fan vids demonstrate that not only Hollywood and comparably vast media networks are capable of producing innovative transmedia projects, as Christy Dena points out. Amateur works like fan vids can also "[get] the best out of the story," (TMSB 2012) exhibiting artistic potential and cultural significance as media texts, even as their creators uphold the DIY ethos and aesthetic independence long associated with the counterculture.

Fan vids epitomize intertextuality across media, celebrating diversification and innovation in storytelling. As Henry Jenkins (2006a) argues, storytelling is "the art of world building," (114) in which artists create a narrative environment that cannot be completely scrutinized or contained within a single work or even a single medium. Such construction complements the "encyclopedia capacity" of digital media, as new-media theorist Janet Murray (1999) suggests, resulting in new narrative modes as viewers seek details beyond the perimeters of the individual stories (253). Such narrative modes will be able to support multiple characters, multiple narratives, and multiple motifs. While some fans see the *Matrix* films, for instance, as appealingly familiar retellings of religious myths, for other fans, the narrative conveys far more than affirmations of received doctrines. Vidders thus allude not only to the Judeo-Christian Messiah myth, but to a range of cultural systems normally considered outside or even irrelevant to it, illustrated b their mashups of *Matrix* footage with sonic backdrop of their own choosing. The reworked story structure engenders complexity, broadening the array of narrative options beyond a linear conduit marked by a beginning, middle, and end. Rather than helping viewers to "grasp the dense psychological and cultural spaces without becoming disoriented" (Murray 1999: 235), fan vids operate in an increasingly fragmented and multicultural context in which users add their own inflections to the movie story, yielding a narrative that may seem less immediately convincing and comprehensible than the original.

In Robert Stam's (1988) analysis, "In the broadest sense, intertextuality [...] refers to the open-ended possibilities generated by all the discursive practices of a culture, the entire matrix of communicative utterances within which the artistic text is situated, and which reach the text not only through recognizable influences but also through a subtle process of dissemination." (138) While traditional media like film certainly permit such open-ended interpretive possibilities, new media technologies expand the range through ever more pervasive dissemination. Within this intertextual matrix, vidders forge popular composites of disparate textual components, displacing them from the coherent narratives in which they were previously embedded. Favorite movie scenes are brought into dialogue with other texts, facilitating multilevel interactions between texts, between users, and between users and texts.

As a vernacular transmedia practice, fan vids offer new information to the knowledge communities we inhabit in the new media age. These knowledge communities are structured around the concept of collective intelligence, the democratic notion that nobody knows everything but everybody knows something, and thus we all depend on each other to gain and share additional information, in Pierre Levy's (1997) formulation. Vidders' creative output can enrich fan-based knowledge communities, even in cases where such contributions were not originally intended. As these communities navigate a complicated information environment, network members pool their knowledge to "build a collective concordance on the Internet." (Jenkins 2006a: 217) They work together not to solve a problem, but to extend the frontier of a narrative, exploring new signifying possibilities in the communicative matrix. Through such collaborative efforts, the depth and breadth of *The Matrix* universe is opened up for exploration not just by individual viewers, but the cyber-community as a whole: a community of audiences who are engaged, confident, capable, and expressive in telling stories in their own ways. Their collaborations attest to the ongoing transformations in the practice of storytelling in an unprecedentedly synergistic, networked global environment.

REFERENCES

Belton, J. (2006). *American Cinema/American Culture*. New York: McGraw-Hill.

Bordwell, D. (1985). *The Classical Hollywood Cinema: Film Style and Mode of Production to 1960*. New York: Columbia University Press.

_____ . (2007). "New Media and Old Storytelling." May 13. http://www.davidbordwell.net/blog/2007/05/13/new-media-and-old-storytelling/. Accessed June 24, 2014

Burgess, J. and Green, J. (2009). *YouTube: Online Video and Participatory Culture*. Cambridge; Malden, MA: Polity.

Campbell, J. (1998). *The Power of Myth*. NY: Doubleday.

Coppa, F. (2006). "Media Fan Fiction as Theatrical Performance," in K. Hellekson and K. Busse (Eds.), *Fan Fiction and Fan Communities in the Age of the Internet* (pp. 225–244). Jefferson, NC: McFarland.

_____ . (2008). "Women, *Star Trek,* and the early development of fannish viding." *Transformative Works and Cultures*. Vol 1. http://journal.transformativeworks.org/index.php/twc/article/view/44/64. Accessed July 3, 2014.

Coyle, J. (2008), "The Best Fan-Made Music Videos on YouTube," *Associated Press*, January 15. http://www.capecodonline.com/apps/pbcs.dll/article?AID=/20080118/LIFE/801180307/-1/rss11. Accessed July 1, 2014.

Davenport, G., S. Agamanolis, B. Barry, B. Bradley and K. Brooks. (2000). "Synergistic Storyscapes and Constructionist Cinematic Sharing." *IBM Systems Journal* 39(3–4): 456–69. http://ic.media.mit.edu/Publications/Journals/Synergistic/HTML/. Accessed July 21, 2014.

Fierman, D. (2003), "The Neo Wave." *Entertainment Weekly*. Time Warner, May 12. http://www.ew.com/ew/article/0,,450805,00.html. Accessed July 2, 2014.

Grist, D. (2013). "Ecclesiastes and Existentialism." *Iron Ink*. http://ironink.org/2013/02/ecclesiastes-and-existentialism/. Accessed June 11, 2014.

Jenkins, H. (2006a). *Convergence Culture: Where Old and New Media Collide*. New York: New York University Press.

_____ . (2006b). "How to Watch a Fan-Vid." September 18, http://henryjenkins.org/2006/09/how_to_watch_a_fanvid.html. Accessed June 11, 2014.

_____ . (2011). 'Transmedia 202: Further Reflections.' August 1. http://henryjenkins.org/2011/08/defining_transmedia_further_re.html. Accessed June 4, 2014.

Kinder, M. (1991). *Playing with Power in Movies, Television, and Video Games: From Muppet Babies to Teenage Mutant Ninja.* Berkeley: University of California Press.

Levy, P. (1997). *Collective Intelligence: Mankind's Emerging World in Cyberspace*. New York: Plenum Trade.

Lothian, A. (2009). "Living in a Den of Thieves: Fan Video and Digital Challenges to Ownership." *Cinema Journal* 48(4).

Murray, J. (1999). *Hamlet on the Holodeck: The Future of Narrative in Cyberspace*. Cambridge, Mass.: MIT Press.

Philips, A. (2012). *A Creator's Guide to Transmedia Storytelling: How to Captivate and Engage Audiences across Multiple Platforms*. New York: McGraw Hill.

Ruppel, M. (2006). Many Houses, Many Leaves: Cross-Sited Media Productions and the Problems of Convergent Narrative Networks. Paper presented at *Digital Humanities 2006 Conference*, July 4–9, Paris-Sorbonne.

Russo, J. L. (2009). "User-Penetrated Content: Fan Video in the Age of Convergence." *Cinema Journal* 48(4): 125-130.

Rutledge, P. (Date Unknown). "Transmedia Storytelling Workshops for Organizations, Branding and Marketing." http://athinklab.com/transmedia-storytelling/what-is-transmedia-storytelling/. Accessed June 10, 2014.

Stam, R. (1988), "Mikhail Bakhtin and Left Cultural Critique," in *Postmodernism and Its Discontents: Theories, Practices*, E. Ann Kaplan (Ed.). London: Verso, pp. 116-145.

Stucky, M. D. (2006). "The Superhero's Mythic Journey: Death and the Heroic Cycle in *Superman." Journal of Religion and Film 10(2). http://www.unomaha.edu/jrf/Vol10No2/Stucky_Superman.htm*. Accessed June 5, 2014.

TMSB (2012), "Transmedia Storytelling around the World: Christy Dena." February 29. http://www.transmedia-storytelling-berlin.de/2012/02/transmedia-storytelling-around-the-world-christy-dena/. Accessed June 30, 2014.

Vogler, C. (1992). *The Writer's Journey.* Cali.: Michael Wiese Productions.
Walker, J. (2004). "Distributed Narrative: Telling Stories Across Networks." Presented at AoIR 5.0. Brighton.
Wikipedia: Fanzine. (Date Unknown), http://en.wikipedia.org/wiki/Fanzine. Accessed June 3, 2014.
Wikipedia: I Against I. (Date Unknown), http://en.wikipedia.org/wiki/I_Against_I. Accessed June 4, 2014.
YouTube Statistics (Date Unknown), http://www.youtube.com/yt/press/statistics.html. Accessed June 15, 2014.

INDEX

#

A

B

D

E

F

G

H

I

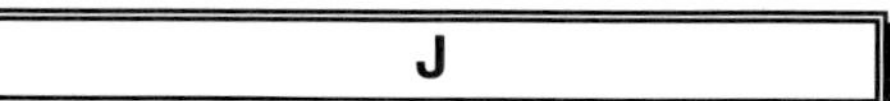

J

K

L

M

N

O

P

R

S

T

U

V

W

Y